A Theatre Geek's Guide to
Disney, Google, and the NFL

Advance Praise for *A Theatre Geek's Guide to Disney, Google, & the NFL*

"Brett N. Axler leads us on an honest and sometimes self-deprecating journey as a knowledgeable tour guide, navigating readers through the straits of career advancement. With comedy, empathy, and common sense, this is a great read for those embarking on their voyage into the work force."

~ **Robert Alberino**, NFL Executive and award-winning storyteller

"Brett Axler provides an incredibly comprehensive, actionable guide that leads its readers through the complex, often confusing maze of career advancement. His upbeat, refreshing perspective makes it easy for anyone to follow, and should be a must-read for anyone looking to progress further towards their dream career goals."

~ **Graham Stephan**, Entrepreneur and YouTube Personality

"Brett has done an excellent job of taking his many professional and personal experiences and woven a story that is insightful and entertaining. His story takes you through the highlights and lowlights of his high school, college, and career experiences. Best of all, Brett explains how he created his own luck, and what he learned from the more difficult moments. If you are starting your career, or looking for a change, Brett's approach to life will help you think of how to move forward, and more importantly to keep moving forward."

~ **Dan Cockerell,** Magic Kingdom, Vice President (Retired)

"Brett has written a must read for every dreamer, ambitious young professional who wants to know the secrets to success and how roadblocks are only a redirection for your career."

~ **Ricki Wax**, Author of *99 Prompts to Mindfulness & Well-Being*

"This is the consummate instruction manual for generating personal career growth in the information age. Brett does a fantastic job of bringing together the age-old skills of networking and knowledge-building with the 21st century skills of self-marketing and leveraging technology to grow your career."

~ **Esteban Morales,** Google, Technical Lead

A Theatre Geek's
Guide to
Disney,
Google, &
the NFL

*What It Takes to Land a Job
with the World's Most
Sought-After Companies*

BRETT N. AXLER

NEW YORK

LONDON • NASHVILLE • MELBOURNE • VANCOUVER

A Theatre Geek's Guide to Disney, Google, and the NFL

What it Takes to Land a Job with the World's Most Sought-After Companies

© 2022 Brett N. Axler

Published in New York, New York, by Morgan James Publishing. Morgan James is a trademark of Morgan James, LLC. www.MorganJamesPublishing.com

ISBN 9781631954863 paperback
ISBN 9781631954870 eBook
Library of Congress Control Number: 2021930444

Cover & Interior Design by:
Christopher Kirk
www.GFSstudio.com

Disclaimer:

I have tried to recreate events, locales, and conversations from my memories of them. In some instances, in order to maintain anonymity, I have changed the names of individuals along with their titles and place of work. All of the opinions in this book are solely those of the author. All of the examples that name companies I have interacted with, interviewed for, or was employed by are only named for the purposes of the lessons this book is supposed to teach. I have a strong respect for every employer or company I name, whether or not they hired me, and whether or not I enjoyed my time partnering with them. I do not intend to cast a poor light on any individual or employer. For that reason, some names and details have been altered or left out entirely.

Morgan James is a proud partner of Habitat for Humanity Peninsula and Greater Williamsburg. Partners in building since 2006.

Get involved today! Visit
MorganJamesPublishing.com/giving-back

Table of Contents

A Note from the Director ix

Chapter 1: Why Me? 1
Chapter 2: The Sound of Music Man, Joseph, and the
            Technical Theatre Dream 13
Chapter 3: Weddings, Bar Mitzvahs, and Proms, oh my 25
Chapter 4: Skill Building Doesn't End with Functional Skills. . 39
Chapter 5: Burnout (On Stress and Anxiety) 55
Chapter 6: Lights, Camera, Football? (On Discovering
            Opportunities You Never Knew Existed) 73
Chapter 7: Physically Not Enough Hours in a Day (On Time
            Management and Learning to Say No) 95
Chapter 8: You Want It? Go and Get It! (On Thinking Outside
            the Box) 105
Chapter 9: You're Never Going to Fly If You Don't Take
            the Leap (On Risky Decisions). 125
Chapter 10: Stepping Down in Rank to Move Up in Company . . 137
Chapter 11: Dreams Take Hard Work to Come True 147
Chapter 12: Only You Know What's Best for You. 157
Chapter 13: Don't Fight the Writing on the Wall 167
Chapter 14: LinkedIn Unleashes Its True Powers 175
Chapter 15: The Importance of a Strong Professional Network. . 187
Chapter 16: Passion is Your Most Powerful Tool. 201
Chapter 17: Company Meeting 207

Curtain Call: It Takes a Community. 219
About the Author 221

A Note from the Director

I'd like to start with a heartfelt thank you.

Thank you for taking the time to read my book and listen to what I have to say. Life is short, and you should always choose how you spend your time wisely, so I appreciate that you have chosen to spend this time with me. For the past few years of my career, I've had friends, family, and coworkers ask when I was going to write my book. I have to admit that just a few years ago, my response to that question was a pretty deep laugh. I was never much of a reader until my mid-twenties, and my grammar is absolutely horrific to this day, but I've gotten pretty far in my life and my career, so I think I'm doing okay.

People have been asking me to write a book about professional networking and career growth for a while now. I never really considered myself as more than an ordinary young professional, but when everyone from Disney executives to Google recruiters raised their eyebrows at my career journey, I started to get on board with the idea that maybe I do have some knowledge and useful experiences to share. My number one hesitation remains the same though: I believe I am very young. I still have a ton to learn myself, and, most importantly, I'm just getting started.

As I write this book, I am twenty-seven years old working for Google in Silicon Valley. If just two years ago my most trusted confidant (or even my clone claiming to be me from the future) told me I would be a Project Manager at Google, living in California, after having left Disney, I would have burst out laughing *(but, actually, I almost didn't even respond to the Google recruiter who first reached out to me because I thought it was a spam message)*. Only a year before that my reaction would have also included me asking what a project manager was. Three years before that, I likely would have responded, "Wait, did you say Disney?"

If there's been one recurring lesson in my life, it has been that life moves incredibly fast and in completely unexpected ways. While rather short, my career has taken some pretty crazy twists and turns over the past decade with a variety of gigs, jobs, and experiences across the country—and world—I would have never dreamed of in high school or college. Although I try to plan everything and consistently update my one-, five-, and ten-year plans to set myself up to reach my goals, life throws a lot of curveballs. Some seem to rip goals and dreams right out from under you but present completely unexpected new opportunities that push you to places you never dreamed, which is really just another way of saying, "When one door closes, another opens." And, wow, has that been the truth I've experienced over the past decade.

I am beyond thankful for all of the experiences I have had up to this point. Some experiences have been once-in-a-lifetime, amazing experiences I will cherish for the rest of my life, while others were not so great and I struggled to understand why I had to go through them. In the end though, no matter what the experiences were or the impact they had on my life, every last one of them taught me lessons that better prepared me for the future. As Steve Jobs said in his 2005 Commencement speech at Stanford University, "You can't connect the dots looking forward; you can only connect them looking backward."

My genuine hope for this book is that it inspires even just a few students and young professionals to think outside the box and find ways to make themselves stand out, opening up for opportunities they never dreamed to be possible. While there are a ton of talented people on this planet, many of whom are just as good, if not better, than you are, ultimately your success comes down to your ability to stand out and market yourself. The world runs on connections and typically the most well-connected end up being the most successful. You could be the best programmer or engineer in the country, but if you simply submit your resume on Microsoft's website without reaching out or following up, you likely have as slim a chance of landing an interview as the self-taught programmer living in his mom's basement. One of the many recurring lessons in this book is that **you have to learn to speak up and market yourself.**

I am incredibly excited to be sharing the lessons I've learned along my journey and the stories behind them. I genuinely hope you find some of them useful and, if not, at least I can guarantee you some pretty ridiculous and entertaining stories. Please keep in mind that I am a completely unapologetic theatre geek and Disney nerd with a terrible sense of sarcasm, humor, and uncalled-for dad jokes and this book absolutely reflects that.

As I mention throughout the book, I have been mentoring students and young professionals for quite a few years now. I absolutely love meeting new people and helping others chart a plan to chase their career goals. I would love to hear from you. Please feel free to check out my website, send me a message, or follow me on LinkedIn.

Now buckle up and keep all hands, arms, and legs inside the book at all times, because you've boarded the wildest ride in the entertainment, media, and sports broadcasting industries.

Chapter 1:

Why Me?

W hy am I writing this book? More specifically, why am I writing this book in my late twenties, just a few years into my professional career? What gives me the right to pose myself as some type of expert people should listen to?

To be honest, those are the same questions that weighed me down for the past year since I started trying to convince myself to write this book. As I mentioned in the director's note, I've had friends, family, and coworkers asking me to write a book. Of course, friends and family would ask to be supportive. After all, they're friends and family. I would hope they would be supportive of my career, and I appreciate that they're impressed with what I've accomplished. But coworkers, professors, and bosses ... why were they asking if I was planning to write a book and share my career insights?

The more I thought about it, the more I realized how much I was already sharing my career insights. I have met with dozens of college students and young professionals seeking career advice. Most were looking for insight into what internships they should focus on in college or asking how they could improve their resume and cover letter to land an interview, but no matter who they were or where they were in their career, they all had at least one thing in common: They were seeking advice from someone they looked up to as an established professional. I could not be more flattered that they thought of me that way.

I absolutely love having those conversations and coaching sessions. I am honored that people of any age or at any stage in their career come to me for advice, but I love meeting with aspiring professionals most of all. And that's who this book is for. It wasn't that long ago that I was in high school dreaming of being a technical director on Broadway or working for Disney, and I was running out of people to ask for advice. Any time I ran into someone who was remotely connected to where I wanted to be, I was thrilled and beyond thankful when they would take time out of their busy schedules to give me advice.

 DiRECTOR's NOTE:
Always make time to return the favor and give to others what was given to you. A simple conversation for you may mean the world to somebody else.

While many of those conversations with industry professionals likely weren't anything special to them, for me, those conversations were groundbreaking moments that I clearly remember to this day. There are a few of those moments that stick out above the rest as turning points that greatly shaped the course of my career.

As I share the story of my career journey—and the lessons I've learned along the way—I will call out the key lessons that have stuck with me over the years. These are the lessons I have found to be most impactful to both my career and personal life. Take them as you will.

"Ɖɪʀᴇᴄᴛᴏʀ's Nᴏᴛᴇs" are the career lessons and takeaways I have found impactful.

 "**Blocking Notes**" are personal lessons and/or funny occurrences.

 The "**SHOW NOTES**" at the end of each chapter sums up the key takeaways. Feel free to grab a pen, a highlighter, and a stack of sticky notes to mark up the ideas that stand out to you. Or if that's not really your thing, you can always refer back to the Show Notes to review the ideas I highlighted throughout the chapter.

Besides my love of paying it forward, I am all too familiar with how most people who reach out to me for career advice are feeling. As early as grade school, I clearly remember having specific career goals and wanting to ask professionals how they got there. I remember the excitement every time that a professional would take the time to answer my questions and speak about their career. It amped me up and inspired me to keep pushing forward.

Now, as a professional who's worked for the NFL, Disney, and Google, to name a few, I make it my personal goal to take the time to provide career advice to students and young professionals—just like those who took the time to speak to me. While I do not consider myself any form of an expert in the realm of career coaching, I have been around the block a few times and I've learned some amazing lessons along the way. I would be doing a disservice to others not to share.

I also find that being young, still navigating the early years of my career, helps me connect better. As inspiring as it is to hear from an accomplished professional over twenty years into their career, they're a lot less relatable than someone just five to ten years into their career.

Still being in my twenties, I grew up in the same technology-driven time as most of today's high school and college students. I understand the stress that social media and the potential for endless scrolling adds—the pressure to be connected all the time and the seemingly unattainable bars that have been set.

To my younger readers: I hear you. I feel you. I understand. Please, trust me, it gets so much better. We'll get through this together.

***

When I was a junior in high school, my family took a trip to Los Angeles over the summer. Among the other usual LA tourist destinations, we spent a few days in Disneyland. Up to that point, I was pretty settled on studying technical theatre in college with the goal of landing a job as a Technical Director or Lighting Designer on Broadway. I had always been a fan of Disney, but I hadn't been to the parks since I was very young, so I didn't remember them well. During the trip, I spent a ton of time walking the parks and looking at all of the technology, from the lights along Main Street to the hydraulic lifts that supported the show technologies for Fantasmic on the Rivers of America. I was enamored by the details and the sheer size of the technology in the parks. To me, a high schooler who loved touring theatres and event spaces to check out the technology, Disneyland was like one enormous playground (but for a much different reason than in the eyes of most guests).

Loving any and all theatre, I attended as many shows as I could while we were there. I was primarily focused on the big shows, but having worked at Six Flags as an audio and lighting technician, I appreciated even the less complex technologies that supported the simpler shows. The first night we were there, we planned to see Fantasmic. I got to the front of Rivers of America hours before the sun set just to watch the crew transitioning Tom Sawyer Island from daytime guest destination to nighttime performance venue. There were technicians loading pyro on the water, acrobats checking the ropes on Captain Hook's ship, stage managers checking headsets at the front of house console, and, what I found most impressive (Honestly, I still find it just as impressive to this day), the thirty-plus-foot hydraulic lifts emerging from the ground, supporting dozens of lights, audio, and special effects equipment.

I was obsessed with all the choreographed work that went into preparing for this show every single night. It took a small army just to prepare for the show, not to mention the performers and crew who ran the show seven nights a week. I stood in awe imagining what it would be like to work on that crew. Little did I know that about five years later and 3,000 miles away on the other side of the country that's exactly what I would be doing.

That night, my family and I watched the show, and I was absolutely floored. I loved it. All I wanted to do was go back the following night and watch it again. However, fate (and my mother) had different plans. The next morning, we arrived at Disney's California Adventure. This was back when it still had that funny-looking Golden Gate Bridge over the entrance and the park was under heavy construction preparing to transition to its new concept. When we entered the park, my mom picked up a map and entertainment guide. She saw there was a new nightly show taking place as part of the soft opening of the park's new entertainment offerings. I asked what time it was at and of course it conflicted with Fantasmic, which I was not thrilled with.

The brief description of the show described it as a new nighttime spectacular featuring fountains and video. It's not that I was completely uninterested in seeing it, but it sounded like it lacked the magic of a live performance. I had seen similar fountain and light shows and they were just alright. I really wanted to rewatch Fantasmic so I could pay closer attention to elements of the show I had missed the night before.

I hoped to take some inspiration home with me for the designs on my high school's next show.

Despite what I had planned, I ended up following my parents to the new show that night. With the lagoon area still mostly under construction and walls from what would eventually be The Voyage of the Little Mermaid protruding into the viewing area, we were all packed pretty tight against the railing of the lagoon. As I looked out over the dark, empty lagoon, I couldn't wrap my head around the idea of Disney putting on a fountain and light show. Even at that age, I knew that Disney was known for their enormous spectacles that involved groundbreaking technology, fireworks, and, most importantly in my opinion, live performers.

The lights from the other side of the lagoon reflected off the calm, dark water before the pre-show announcement began. As the announcement came to an end, the lights blacked out and half a beat later the classic soundtrack of the 1960s Walt Disney's "Wonderful World of Color" echoed through the lagoon as a small, short rainbow of backlit fountains sprayed to life in a line in the middle of the otherwise dark lagoon. I rolled my eyes in protest to the unenthusiastic opening of the show. But half a second later, the fountains were out, it was pitch black once again, and out of nowhere, a 3D image of Tinker Bell flew across the center of the lagoon trailing pixie dust that spelled "World of Color". My mouth dropped to the ground.

Putting this into perspective, this was 2010. The iPhone had been out for less than two years, HD-TVs were just starting to be standard on the market, and the Nokia Tower 3D show that made projection mapping world-famous was still over a year away from happening. Watching a perfectly video-mapped image of Tinker Bell skirt across a water screen in the middle of a lagoon followed by a perfectly legible trail of video and lasers spelling out "World of Color" was an insanely big deal. As the show carried on for another thirty minutes, I was in absolute awe of the array of perfectly choreographed technologies on display. As soon as the show came to an end, I looked over at my parents and said, "I'm going to work for Disney."

From that moment on, my college and career focus completely shifted from Broadway to Disney. I spent countless hours researching the show's technology, finding out who the design teams were, what third-party vendors were involved, and, most importantly, what I needed to study in college to land a position at Disney working on designing these types of shows. This is where I started to run into problems.

Throughout most of high school I had connections in Broadway and professional theatre to reach out to for advice. I had spent years developing relationships, gaining access to priceless firsthand experience and an inside look into the field I planned to study. Now shifting my focus to Disney, I didn't know anyone who had worked there who could provide me any advice, and I didn't have a clue where I should focus my attention to gain experience. I drove myself and my parents nuts during the college application process because I did not know what I wanted to study. While there were endless opportunities in technical theatre and radio, television, and film programs, I didn't know if any of those programs were what Disney would find desirable in an applicant.

I found every book, article, and video I could get my hands on about working for Disney and the education path that would best set me up to successfully land a job with them. At the time, I would have done anything to even get a fifteen-minute conversation with anyone who had experience working for Disney just to pick their brain for advice. I remember going as far as finding an IAmA article on Reddit published by a former technician at Walt Disney World sharing his experiences working in the parks. While it wasn't very useful advice for an aspiring professional, it was at least some insight into life at Disney.

About a year later, opportunities started to present themselves in the realm of Disney. The first was during my senior year of high school when one of my old bosses moved down to Orlando and started as a

Parade Manager in Magic Kingdom. Luckily, I had stayed in touch with him, and I already had a trip planned to go down there with my high school senior class. I reached out to him and less than three months later I was standing in the middle of the castle hub meeting with my old boss talking all about what steps I could take to make it to Disney. At that point, I had already signed with the college that I was going to attend but I still had so many questions for him.

That was one of the first fifteen-minute career chats that I will never forget. To him, it was just fifteen minutes out of his day speaking to a former employee, but to me, a high schooler getting the chance to talk to a professional in the career I was aspiring toward, it meant the world. (Thanks, Frank!)

Director's Note:
Always stay in touch. Professional networking is just as much about keeping existing connections alive as it is about making new ones. Staying in touch in the twenty-first century is easier than it has ever been before. From a quarterly email or a friendly ping on messenger to posting "Happy Birthday" on an old friend's Facebook feed or sending a holiday card, whatever method you choose is better than losing touch. Personally, I find it a lot nicer to ask or be asked by someone for a connection or lead who I've been in touch with recently than someone who's reaching out to me for the first time in years simply wanting something from me. (I'm looking at you, high school classmates!)

A second opportunity came a few weeks into my freshman year of college, I was sitting in a class where local entertainment and production professionals were invited to speak about their careers. Debbie, a local freelance producer, spoke about her experience working as a producer and stage manager for concerts, events, and parades around Philadelphia and New York City. At the end of the lecture, she mentioned that she was looking for a few volunteers for the Thanksgiving Day Parade. I ran right up to her after the lecture and asked how many volunteers she needed. We exchanged email addresses and, six weeks later, I found myself and five classmates I recruited standing on the parade route at the 6abc Thanksgiving Day Parade as production assistants.

When my team and I arrived that morning, we were told we would be meeting the stage manager at the bottom of the steps of the Philadelphia Museum of Art. (Those are the "Rocky Steps" for all of you unfamiliar with Philly). At 3 a.m. on the dot we met Gene at the foot of the steps. The weather was below freezing, and we were all exhausted. No one had time for introductions before we jumped right into work.

My team and I followed Gene around for the better half of the morning leading up to the parade. He showed us how to follow the script, the various ways he would cue us for the special effects, and what areas to stay out of in order to keep the back of our heads out of the view of the television cameras. By the time the sun started to make its way over the city skyline, the parade had stepped off and Gene had us running around like the Seven Dwarfs placing performers, setting off confetti, clearing set pieces, and keeping the parade moving. It was a blast.

At the end of the parade, the production team gathered to help load the last of the props into the trailers. As we finished loading the last truck, Gene approached the crew and thanked us all for our hard work. He asked if we planned on coming back the following year to help out again. Everyone on the crew gave an enthusiastic nod and Gene smiled, "Great! See you all then! Have a Happy Thanksgiving." As the crew left, Gene and one of the other stage managers held me back to thank me for organizing the volunteers.

They mentioned that their team ran a handful of other parades around the country throughout the year and asked if I was interested in any travel production work. I immediately expressed my interest, and Gene handed me his business card and told me to send him an email with my information. I took a quick look down at the card as I reached out to shake his hand. Mickey Mouse peered up at me holding a cane and a top hat. I quickly took a second look at the card before looking back at Gene.

"You work for Disney?!" I basically screamed.

"Thirty years and counting" he replied.

That was the second fifteen-minute career chat I will never forget.

***

So, what's the point of me sharing these stories? Well, for one, it helps the five of you taking the time to read this book who are not my mother learn more about me. (Again, thank you!) But really, while there are quite a few takeaways from these stories and additional details that I will refer to throughout the book and draw lessons from, the primary focus of this chapter remains: *Why Me?*

As I mentioned before, while I may not be an expert or published professor on the subjects of careers and professional networking, I have found that some of the best guidance and advice provided to me over the years has come from professionals working in the careers that I have spent my life pursuing.

Just like Frank and Gene, along with dozens of other professionals I will call out and thank in this book, took the time to share their two cents with me about how to land my dream jobs and navigate my wild career journey, I am here to do the same for whoever may find my stories useful. I have always been incredibly focused on my career goals, and I have never allowed anyone or anything to stop me from pursuing them.

While I have accomplished a lot, and it's been an amazing journey so far, I have a ton more to do, and I would love to take you all along with me. I'm just getting started.

SHOW NOTES:

- Always take time to return the favor and give to others what was given to you.
- Seek out professionals who are already working in the job or industry that you aspire to work in. Their insights and advice will be the closest you can get to actually being in that job. Listen to what they have to say and don't be afraid to ask questions.
- Keep an open mind when trying to pinpoint what you would like to go to school for or do for a living. For every job out there that sounds interesting to you, there are five more that are an even better fit you have likely never even heard of. Depending on your field of interest, there are many jobs that may be perfect for you that don't even exist yet and are just waiting for you to fill that need.
- Say yes to all opportunities that sound interesting to you. You never know who you may meet and what it may lead to.
- Speak up! Introduce yourself. You never know who the person standing in front of you may be connected to or what experience and insights they may have to offer.
- Out of sight, out of mind. Put just as much effort into staying in touch with your professional connections as you do into meeting new ones.

Chapter 2:

The Sound of Music Man, Joseph, and the Technical Theatre Dream

S o where did this technical theatre dream of mine begin?

I don't know if I am alone in feeling this way, but one of my favorite questions to ask anyone I work with or look up to as a professional is **what initially sparked their interest.** The variety of answers you receive when asking this question a few hundred times across a bunch of creative industries is amazing.

There are, of course, many of the usual answers for those of us in theatre and entertainment that involve starting on stage or in the dance studio as children. Then there are the outliers who didn't discover their love for the arts until high school when they realized that the theatre kids were actually much cooler than expected. Finally, there are the ones who were born into it and know no other life.

The responses from theme park professionals get even more interesting and varied. I've talked to Imagineers who knew they had absolutely no other option than to get themselves into Imagineering after their first trip to Disney as a child and others who had never even been to a Disney theme park until they were hired. I had coworkers in the NFL who grew up working on family farms and worked their way onto the grounds crew after college and others similar to me who worked their whole lives in theatre, never attending a professional football game until they accidentally landed a job there.

No matter what the answer is, I absolutely love asking that question. I find it to be an excellent way to get to know your coworkers and leaders, and I personally find it inspiring to hear about someone who grew up with a dream of being an NBA player and ended up landing in a PhD program for an incredibly fulfilling career after they realized *most* 5'10" guys don't make it to the NBA.

While I genuinely believe that you should never compare yourself to anyone else, I find there is no harm in learning how others got their start. It can spark a bit of inspiration.

That being said, where did it start for me? Well, I can assure you that I absolutely did not grow up expecting to be working at Google in Silicon Valley. To be completely honest, even just a few years ago when the film *The Internship* featuring Vince Vaugh and Owen Wilson came out, my initial reaction to the film was, "It was an okay movie, I could never see myself working for Google though."

Yet here we are.

 Director's Note:
Life works in weird, unexpected ways. Never say never, always keep an open mind, and be willing to try ALMOST anything at least once.

***

For all of my fellow theatre geeks, as you may have already gathered from the title of this chapter, my life started in theatre. Growing up in South Jersey about twenty minutes outside of Philadelphia and forty-five minutes outside of New York City, theatre and the performing arts were very popular in my hometown. There were a ton of community and regional theatres in the area with some of the oldest in the country just in South Jersey, not to mention famous theatres and opera houses in Philadelphia, including The Academy of the Arts, Plays and Players, and the recently reopened Met on North Broad.

My mother has always had a love for musical theatre, so she started taking me to shows when I was in preschool. Other than a few Purim Shpiels at my synagogue, the very first show I saw on stage was *Joseph and the Technicolor Dream Coat*. I had to have only been three or four years old at the time, but I still remember certain scenes from that performance clear as day. Funny enough, other than the music of the show, what I really remember were the special effects. Go figure, even at the age of three I was already into fog and lighting effects.

Over the next few years, my parents took my brother and I to countless shows. I remember seeing *The Jungle Book* at the Arden Theatre, *Nerds the Musical* at Plays and Players, and a variety of children's shows at the Ritz Theatre in Oakland, New Jersey.

I was absolutely hooked. Even at that age, I was inspired by the music, the passion, and the sheer amount of fun it looked like everyone on stage was having.

For my eighth birthday, my parents and grandparents took me to the Bucks County Playhouse to see a community theatre production of *The Music Man*. I remember being so excited to see kids on stage who were my age in what I perceived to be a professional production. That was the day I told my parents I wanted to be in a musical.

***

Blocking Note:

It's been a nice walk down memory lane while writing this chapter. As I mentioned before, life works in weird and unexpected ways. All of the theatres I mentioned I attended shows at as a young child, I have since worked for some capacity (Aside from The Met on North Broad as it was still abandoned when I last worked in Philadelphia). The same goes for each of the shows. I have either been in or worked on every one of those shows since. **The Music Man** in particular, I have been in and worked on four times, and I can't wait for the opportunity to do it again. Although I cannot say the same for my three productions of **Les Misérables**. Great show … but never again. This is another example of how life works in weird ways and you should never rule out any dream.

Throughout grade school, I acted in a number of shows, from *The Music Man* and *Bugsy Malone* to a few watered-down Shakespearean straight plays. Most of it was just as fun as I had hoped, and I honestly didn't have any intention of stopping. Then middle school happened.

Fourth and fifth grade were some really awful years for me. Throughout elementary school I always had my tight group of friends. Growing up in a small township, there were less than sixty kids in my grade, and we all got along pretty well. Other than a few kids that would come and go from the Fort Dix Air Force Base, we were a pretty consistent group during those years. But the summer before I started fourth grade, there was a new neighborhood built in my township. The new neighbors increased the size of my class by almost 30 percent in one summer. When I arrived back at school in September, the dynamic had completely changed.

I still had my small group of friends, but now we were being targeted and there was a small group that began to bully me. It started with the usual childish bullying you would expect to find in any grade school with things like name-calling and mocking. It quickly grew into the same group of students mocking and talking back at the teacher, which for some reason the teacher would respond to with laughter, making them think their actions were acceptable. By the middle of that year, I had spit-filled wads of paper thrown at the back of my head in class and was tripped in the hallway.

Oh, did I mention this was a group entirely of girls?

Every time I reported the problem to my teacher, her response would be something along the lines of, "Oh that's just what girls do when they like you and they're trying to get your attention." Whether that was true or not, it was getting worse, and the school administration wasn't doing anything about it.

That year, I had one of the lead roles in a school play. By that point I had been in quite a few shows and I was confident onstage. One afternoon, our director took us around to all of the fourth- and fifth-grade classrooms to perform a short scene from the show. One of those was my fourth-grade class that, of course, included the group of girls who had been bullying me half the year at that point. The scene went off without a hitch (or as good as you can expect from a bunch of middle schoolers performing at the front of the classroom). But when I returned to class, there were already notes shoved into my desk. Middle schoolers get very creative with the ways they choose to mock fellow classmates.

This was strike one for me. I felt sick to my stomach and it made me question whether I did actually look like a fool standing on stage.

As the weeks went on, the girls continued to write me nasty notes. The notes soon turned into them sitting behind me in music class mocking my singing. Eventually they started vocalizing their dislike for me to the class. I will never forget the day in fourth-grade music class when the self-appointed leader of their group raised her hand.

"Um, excuse me, I can't participate because I can't hear over Brett's terrible singing."

The class burst out laughing as our useless substitute struggled to handle the situation.

This was strike two.

Somehow, I managed to make it through the rest of that year without the drama escalating much further. That summer I continued to act in camp plays, but they were suddenly becoming less fun, and I was getting nervous on stage. The sound of the girls mocking me echoed in my head and the images of their mean notes caused me to believe what they were saying may have been true.

The following year in fifth grade, the bullying got so out of control that my mom actually pulled me out of school a few weeks early. By the end of that year, the girls had turned some of my best friends against me. I later learned that they were threatening my friends by telling them that they would do similar things to publicly humiliate them if they continued to hang out with me.

This was strike three. That year I quit acting onstage, I quit singing in the chorus, and I would have completely quit theatre if not for the saving grace of one of my biggest mentors in life: my band director, Mr. Morgan.

 Blocking Note:

Looking back on the social issues that I had in fourth and fifth grade, they are an example of a rare occurrence in my past I really can't seem to explain the reasons for to this day. While I never have and never will wish or celebrate any harm or misfortune of others (schadenfreude as they refer to it in *Avenue Q*), I did take the time to look up where a few of those girls are now and I will politely say that what goes around, comes around.

I do not have many regrets in life, but quitting acting is one of them. I love speaking in front of crowds, I love to entertain people, and stage fright has never been part of my vocabulary. While I won't call it a goal, a dream of mine is to make it back onstage one day in some capacity.

***

There is a long-standing tradition of instrumental music in my family. Both of my parents and grandfathers played instruments, and I grew up listening to my mom and my grandfather play duets on the piano at my grandparents' house. To this day, those are some of my favorite childhood memories that include my grandparents.

In the Jewish religion, it's customary not to play instruments on the Sabbath and most holidays. My grandfather was a cantor and therefore was very observant. His voice was absolutely mesmerizing, and his skills as a pianist were equally impressive. As a child, most of the nights that my brother and I would spend at my grandparents' house would be during the observance of the Sabbath or holidays, and once the sun set and the Sabbath was over, we didn't want to disturb the neighbors. This didn't leave many opportunities to hear my mother and grandfather play, so when they did, it was a special occasion.

I loved listening to my grandfather play, and when my mom sat down next to him, my brother and I knew we were not going anywhere. Between my mom having played piano since she was a child and my grandfather's innate ability to play by ear, the two of them would never repeat the same routine twice. As the two of them would sing and play, bouncing tunes off each other, feeding on one another's energy, my brother, dad, and grandmother would sit on the couch and listen in awe. This quickly led to my interest in learning to play an instrument at a young age. Not having a piano in our house as a kid, I was always told

I would be learning to play an instrument in middle school, and fifth grade music came just in time.

Mr. Morgan was the school's instrumental music teacher. He was well-known in the community as an absolutely amazing music teacher, and his reputation fell short of his true talents. As a teacher, musician, mentor, and all-around amazing, kind-hearted person, Mr. Morgan still stands out as one of the most influential people in my life. He had no idea that he came into my life at a crucial time.

When asked what instrument I wanted to play, I had no doubt that I wanted to play trumpet. My grandfather had played the bugle in the army, and he knew how to play trumpet because it was very similar. I think this was what initially led to my interest in playing the instrument. Beyond that, I just loved the sound of the trumpet. I loved that it could carry itself in such a wide variety of genres. It was my goal from day one to learn to play the national anthem so I could perform at the opening of one of the school's basketball games.

I ended up playing trumpet all through middle school into my freshman year of high school when I joined the brass line in the marching band. Through those years, I fell in love with music, and for a few years I wanted to be a music teacher just like Mr. Morgan. I was told that I would need to learn a wide variety of instruments in order to be a music teacher, so Mr. Morgan took the time to teach me the basics of the French horn and tuba, and, on the side, I started learning the baritone and piano. I also learned to write sheet music and combined my love for music and technology when I had the chance to get a copy of Finale, an early software package for the digital scribing of sheet music that even played an 8-bit version of the notes back to you.

***

Aside from music, my grade school years were the years I really started to dive into technology. I grew up on computers from a very young age. Both of my parents have worked their entire lives in computers, as did my grandfather back in the sixties. With my dad as a software engineer and my mom in computer sales back in the eighties, our home had a computer with internet access in the early nineties.

As early as kindergarten I remember sitting with my dad at the computer. He would check to make sure that no one was on the phone, then he would click the dial-up button. For any of you who were actually old enough during those years to remember dial-up, you're likely hearing the classic soundtrack in your head right now of your computer connecting to the world wide web.

My friends and I spent most of our childhoods on computers. *Paint* and *Art Studio* on Windows 95 turned into *Oregon Trail* and *Rollercoaster Tycoon* on Windows 2000, which quickly led to *AIM, LimeWire, and RuneScape*. The nineties and early 2000s were a different time to grow up on computers. By the time I got to middle school I was already well versed in HTML-based web design and knew the work-arounds to get past my classroom's teacher-control software. Luckily, I was pretty close with my computer teacher, so I stayed out of trouble for the most part.

In sixth grade I started my first blog and in seventh grade my first website. My friends and I loved playing free games online, but by sixth grade the school's firewall was improving and blocked most of the gaming websites. I soon figured out that it only blocked web addresses and content keywords, so I built my own website that made it past the school's firewall and embedded all of my friend's favorite games. That worked for about two days before our computer teacher, Mr. DJ, caught on and then my website was quickly blocked.

This got the school's attention though. By eighth grade I was the go-to guy for all things websites, and I ended up designing a class website for my civics class. This was my first time using a WYSIWYG web designer, and I discovered that the platform allowed the integration of Google AdSense. I signed up for an AdSense account and embedded ads to generate income from the class website. The only flaw with my plan was that all of the hits on the website were coming from the same gateway and AdSense soon shut down my account. *(While I couldn't collect any of the money then, I think it worked out pretty well with a sign-on bonus working for the parent company fifteen years later.)*

***

Other than being a fantastic music teacher and mentor who led me through my tough middle school years, there was an even larger positive impact Mr. Morgan had on me. He kick-started my interest in audio and technical theatre.

Around the same time that I quit acting on stage and singing in chorus, I discovered a small, powered audio system in my school's cafeteria. Having been in quite a few shows, I always had some curiosity about how audio systems worked, but I never really had anyone to ask. Mr. Morgan would always set up the audio system before our school's shows and concerts, so I asked him if he could teach me how to set up and run it. After a quick overview of where all the wires went and what each knob did, I was hooked. From then on, I was the school's audio guy. Every concert, show, PTA meeting, and back to school night, I was there, running the audio system.

Before long I was getting asked to run audio for events around town—the community's Memorial Day celebration, our Halloween hayride and bonfire event, and our annual community day. Being such a small township, word spread fast. It wasn't long before running audio turned into DJing (which at that time was basically just playing a list of songs from iTunes or the early version of the iPod). But these experiences quickly led to discovering of the opportunities that DJing had to offer.

I found that DJing scratched a few itches for me: my love for technology, music, and entertainment. The experience gave me a platform to practice my skills while growing new ones, it got my name out in the community, opening new opportunities for gigs and to meet people, and it gave me a really good excuse to purchase and play with new technology.

The only problem was that getting started was very expensive.

 ## SHOW NOTES:

- Life works in weird, unexpected ways. Never say never, always keep an open mind, and be willing to try *ALMOST* anything at least once.
- You never know how your skills and interests may overlap to create new opportunities for you. Be open-minded, build up as many skills as you can, and always be on the lookout for new opportunities.
- Ask questions! If you're curious about how something works, ask someone, look it up online or watch a tutorial on YouTube. It may just lead to you discovering a new hobby or career path.
- When you're young, you tend to have a ton of time on your hands. Take advantage of it and try as many new things as possible.

Chapter 3:

Weddings, Bar Mitzvahs, and Proms, oh my

For DJing school and community events, I was able to borrow the school's equipment. When events got a little more complicated, I would partner with the local DJs in the community who were more established and were nice enough to allow me to borrow some of their spare equipment. Ultimately though I was hitting my boundaries for the events I was able to take on because I did not have the computer or music library to pull off the larger events. This was 2006 when there weren't any streaming services, and I could only download so many songs on LimeWire per hour with a DSL internet connection.

But then the stars seemed to align at a family event. My cousin had been a long-time DJ in the Delaware Valley. His days as a DJ started with him carrying crates of records to each gig. The records were eventually upgraded to tapes and, by the time I met him, racks of CDs. He had a well-established company with a crew of guys and multiple sets of equipment. I got to talking with him about the technology I was using to DJ some of the school and community events. I explained how digitizing the music defeated the purpose of burning new CDs every month, carrying around those CDs to every event, and knowing exactly where to find each song. He was intrigued but had some concerns. Like most business owners who are comfortable with the way things work, he didn't want to alter a process that had been working well for him for a long time.

I continued to follow up with him the next few months until he finally allowed me to shadow one of his events. He told me I was just there to be a fly on the wall and see how his guys worked, but I decided to come prepared with equipment anyway. The party was an afternoon bar mitzvah. As most afternoon events are, it was a snooze. It's hard to make a crowd dance at a dressy event on a Saturday afternoon, especially after they all got up early, rushed to synagogue, and sat through a three-hour service. The kids at the event didn't make starting the party much easier. The group mostly consisted of nerdy pre-adolescent boys who were more interested in playing their Gameboys and wouldn't be caught dead on the dance floor. It was a losing battle. Eventually my cousin's DJ walked up to the kid whose bar mitzvah it was and asked what he wanted to listen to. As I expected, his response was not the Top 40 pop music of the early 2000s.

Like most of my friends at that age, he and his friends were video game nerds who were into the niche genres they had discovered playing their RPGs and simulation games. The DJ looked dumbstruck. He had never heard any of the music the boy was talking about, and he definitely didn't have it in his library of CDs that spanned from seventies rock through 2K pop. Being the nerdy, overprepared teenager that I was, I rolled my eyes and pulled out my laptop. Some of the songs I already had in iTunes and the others I quickly downloaded. I handed my laptop to the DJ, we plugged it into his mixer, and, voila, happy pre-teens.

As expected, at the end of the party, my cousin and his DJ approached me about the technology.

"Alright, it's time. What do we need?"

Director's Note:
Be patient and be prepared. Not every opportunity will come quickly or when expected, but when it does present itself, make sure you are prepared to take the bull by the horns and give it all you've got.

Over the next couple of months, I worked with my cousin and his staff to pick out laptops and external hard drives and showed them how to rip CDs and import them into the software. We tested out a few different pieces of DJ software but in 2007 our options were limited. Luckily, we were able to partner with another local DJ company to lessen the effort required to rip tens of thousands of songs from CDs and import and organize them in the software.

By the end of 2007, we had gone fully digital.

Although I had the technical expertise to upgrade the team's technology and train them on how to use it, I was still only fourteen years old and didn't have much DJ experience. While it was cool to have a local student DJ the community events, having a fourteen-year-old on staff for bar mitzvahs and weddings wasn't the most professional look. It was next to impossible for me to understand at that age, but luckily my cousin was patient with me and continued to find ways to fit me in.

Director's Note:
As a student or young professional, you may not always understand the reasoning for every decision. Sometimes it may be not enough experience or insight to see the whole picture. When you are new to a job, go in quiet as

a lamb with the ears of a rabbit and be patient as a monk. Patience young Padawan, your time will come.

By the end of eighth grade, my calendar was booked solid. My cousin helped me purchase my first set of professional DJ equipment and I was off to the races. Around the same time, I got my braces off, lost the glasses, and started to grow into my face, so it was hard to tell my age. The following years were a whirlwind of events. From weddings and bar mitzvahs to graduation parties and community days, I was busy every single weekend.

I was learning how to talk to clients, network in the DJ and entertainment community, and advertise my work. It wasn't long before I started integrating my other interests into my work like social media, web design, and video production. We were one of the first DJ companies in the area to offer music videos, cocktail hour gaming systems, and platforms for the hosts to show video montages.

As we started to expand and a few of my cousin's staff DJs left to head off to college, we began looking for help and I ended up bringing in my buddy Josh from school. He didn't have any experience as a DJ, but he knew his music and he was incredibly professional for his age. While Josh fit right in, he brought another incredibly useful talent with him that none of us expected. Women of all ages absolutely loved him. Any event he would work with us, there would be girls flocking to the DJ booth to talk to him. He would flash a smile and receive napkins with phone numbers. Even the grandmothers loved him! It was a sight to behold.

Being the nerdy, unpopular teenager, I was definitely jealous of Josh's charisma and ability to attract girls, and I did a pretty poor job of hiding my frustration until we turned sixteen and I realized the market value of having someone like Josh on the team. There were weekends we were on the verge of turning down events because of the sheer number of sweet sixteen parties we were getting asked to DJ.

Dïrector's Note:

Don't ignore your frustrations. They may just lead to your next big idea or opportunity. Why did Walt Disney create Disneyland? He was tired of sitting on a park bench watching his daughters play. He wanted a place where he and his daughters could have fun together. Why did Steve Jobs create the iPhone? Why did Mark Zuckerberg create Facebook? Why did Elon Musk risk his entire career and fortune building Tesla and SpaceX?

It was around this same time that I started having clients reach out about production work. While the DJ business was going well with my cousin, audio visual production was a parallel business that did not really fit into the DJ company's vision or public image. As I started to take those jobs, they quickly led to larger events that required liability insurance and more complex contracts. At the ripe age of sixteen, I founded my first LLC: *Action Packed Productions and Entertainment.*

Dïrector's Note:

You are never too young or inexperienced to be an entrepreneur. Of course, as a minor, you may have to get a parent or guardian to cosign legally, but with the world at your fingertips, you can have your own LLC (limited liability company) registered in minutes. My personal belief is that the younger you start, the better. You have energy, enthusiasm, time on your hands, and hopefully the world hasn't beaten you down too bad yet, so you're generally more optimistic. When you're young you also have less to lose and are less afraid to fail. Think of how many businesses started in the founder's parents' or friends' garages (Hewlett Packard, Google, and Apple, just to name a few).

This was the production company that allowed me to advertise and take on events outside of DJ work. From school plays to audio system upgrades in local theatres, business ramped up quickly. Every time my buddies and I ran an event, word of mouth spread and led to three or four new events. Before long we were being hired by all of the local schools, churches, and municipalities to provide audio for their events, record video, and provide DVD and digital publishing services.

Being a group of teenage guys with an abnormal number of connections across the Delaware Valley, we kept ourselves busy. There were weekends between March and July we were getting asked to work up to five events in two days. By junior year of high school, the business had gotten so busy that we were subcontracting the work to other companies, most of which were owned and operated by professionals twice our age. We would hire our high school video production teacher to take care of any video work that came in, any larger events like weddings and bar mitzvahs we would do a white label contract with my cousin's company, and we would keep all of the fun events for ourselves like proms and sweet sixteens.

There was one year that we had the contracts for four high school proms on the same weekend and every single person who worked for us was supposed to attend one of those proms. I ended up hiring a former coworker of mine to take care of two of the proms and had to pair up my buddies based on their levels of experience to cover the other proms while I too attended one of those proms as a guest.

By the time we were all heading off to college, we had almost completely outsourced all of our events and client engagements to other companies in order to focus on the most important years of our lives to come. Outsourcing the events soon led to turning over the contracts completely and by the end of my freshman year of college, I liquidated the company in order to focus on school and the new ventures I'll tell you about shortly. In the end, it was a tough decision to shut down the company but not one I ever regretted.

My years as a teenage entrepreneur taught me endless lessons in business, leadership, taxes, contracts, negotiation, problem solving, scalability, and finance. These are all lessons that I am confident no other job would have taught me by the age of eighteen. I am forever thankful that I had those amazing opportunities at such a young age, and I guarantee the lessons I learned along the way played a huge part in my future success in the corporate world.

I highly recommend that every driven teen or young adult with an idea just go for it. Start the business, write the blog, build the contraption, market your services—you've got nothing to lose.*

> *Footnote: While I say with confidence "you've got nothing to lose," please be smart and don't do anything reckless or stupid. Sean Parker may have made a name for himself with Napster, but he was quickly sued by every record label followed by anyone who's ever attended the Grammys (Thanks for the quote, Justin Timberlake).

Historically while telling this story, there are a few common questions I get that I am sure many of you are wondering about as well.

How did a bunch of high schoolers find the time to run a DJ and production company on top of being full-time high school students?

This is a question I get asked about my life and schedule management skills even to this day from my boss at Google. There are twenty-four hours in a day. When you track how you are spending each of those twenty-four hours, you would be amazed at how much time most people waste when they could be spending it more productively. Here's a sample of what my average day of high school looked like:

- *5:15 a.m. Wake up and get ready*
- *6:00 a.m. Breakfast with my dad at home*
- *6:30 a.m. Dad drops me off at school on his way to work*
- *6:30–7:30 a.m. Finish homework*
- *7:30–8:00 a.m. School activity (Tech Crew, TV Club, Morning News)*
- *8:00 a.m.–2:30 p.m. Classes*
- *2:30–4:30 p.m. Seasonal tech rehearsals or theatre tech crew*
- *4:30–6:00 p.m. Return client calls and emails, dinner, and homework*
- *6:00–9:00 p.m. Musical rehearsals, AV for school meetings and events*
- *9:00–11:00 p.m. Homework, study, company contracts, and scheduling*
- *11:00 p.m. Sleep*

Out of every twenty-four hours, Monday through Friday, I was being productive or taking care of life's necessities for about seventeen of those hours. What don't you see on that list? Watching TV, playing video games, getting in trouble with friends, hanging out with a girlfriend, and being a generally moronic teenager wasting life away. I did not waste any time in high school. I knew what I wanted from a young age, and I was not going to let a busy schedule or time-wasting activities get in the way.

As you would expect, my weekends consisted of working on DJ and production company business around the clock. There were weekends that were so packed I had to hire set and strike crews. If I had a Saturday afternoon bar mitzvah in Cherry Hill followed by a wedding in Philadelphia that evening, I would hire a crew to set up the DJ equipment for the wedding while I was DJing the bar mitzvah, then I would head out to DJ the wedding and that crew would come strike the equipment from the bar mitzvah.

Director's Note:
Choose how you spend your time wisely. You will be amazed how much you can accomplish when you make the effort to plan out your daily schedule and avoid unnecessary distractions like television and video games.

How did so many clients trust a bunch of high schoolers with their events and life celebrations?

The funniest thing about this question is that I am still wondering the same thing myself to this day. When I was in middle school DJing weddings and bar mitzvahs, no one ever said a thing to me about my age. When I was a freshman in high school running audio at Six Flags, no one ever asked my age. When I hand-delivered contracts to clients, schools, or municipalities for DJ and production work, no one ever asked my age. Even when I was fifteen years old attending parties at the clubs in Atlantic City during the National DJ Convention, no one ever asked my age.

Looking back on all of the crazy experiences I had at a very young age, there are definitely quite a few situations I still have to ask myself how in the world I ever got away with it. Ultimately, I believe there were two primary factors that helped me land those opportunities without any questions: **Confidence and reputation.**

Director's Note:
Be confident in what you know and don't know. No one knows everything. No matter how young or inexperienced you may be, odds are you know a lot more about a certain topic or skill than most other people.

Director's Note:
Reputation is everything. It takes time to build trust, but once people like and trust you enough to tell their friends

and professional connections about you, your name will spread like wildfire. Nothing beats word-of-mouth advertising. Beware: This rule goes both ways though. Don't let your reputation precede you in a negative light.

 Dırector's Note:
The world runs on personal connections. Whether you're referred by a former client to their friend, referred by an alumnus on a college application, or referred by a current employee on a job application, the odds will almost always be on your side when you have a personal connection. Meet people, grow your network, and always stay in touch. You'll see throughout this book how many times that has worked out for me throughout my career.

Was the company profitable?

Yes, but purposely no. As much as I have always loved earning, saving, and spending money, the goal of my DJ and production business in high school was never to make money. I learned to DJ in middle school because I thought it looked like a lot of fun (and it was). I learned to run audio and lighting for events in high school because I thought that was fun too (still is fun!). Both of those lines of business required a ton of really expensive gear that I couldn't easily get my hands on as a teenager, so I had to purchase the equipment myself. Luckily, researching, purchasing, learning/using, then reselling the equipment was also a hobby of mine. The business made quite a bit of money. I paid my contractors (friends) quickly and fairly, put a little bit in savings, then reinvested the rest back into the business in equipment purchases and upgrades. I believe I operated the business at a loss every year. While I walked away with a little bit of cash for college, the money wasn't where the true value was. By the time I entered college, I had already had almost six years of professional DJ and production experience and almost four years of experience as an entrepreneur. Most importantly, my professional network by the age of seventeen spanned six states and two countries.

Director's Note:
Know the true value of every experience. While many experiences in school and early in your career may not pay a lot, the opportunity cost usually makes up for it. Take advantage of these opportunities as ways to learn, grow your skills, and broaden your professional network.

Show Notes:

- As a student or young professional, you may not always understand the reasoning for every decision. Sometimes it may have to do with not having enough experience or insight to see the whole picture. When you are new to a job, go in quiet as a lamb with the ears of a rabbit and be patient as a monk.
- Don't ignore your frustrations. They may just lead to your next big idea or opportunity. Use them as inspiration to solve the problem.
- You are never too young or inexperienced to be an entrepreneur. Of course, as a minor, you may have to get a parent or guardian to cosign legally, but with the world at your fingertips, you can have your own LLC (limited liability company) registered in minutes. My personal belief is that the younger you start the better. You have energy, enthusiasm, time on your hands, and hopefully

the world hasn't beaten you down too bad yet, so you're generally more optimistic. When you're young, you also have less to lose and are generally less scared to fail.

- Choose how you spend your time wisely. You will be amazed at how much you can accomplish when you make the effort to plan out your daily schedule and avoid unnecessary distractions like television and video games.
- Be confident in what you know and don't know. No one knows everything. No matter how young or inexperienced you may be, odds are you know a lot more about a certain topic or skill than most other people.
- Reputation is everything. It takes time to build trust, but once people like and trust you enough to tell their friends and professional connections about you, your name will spread like wildfire. Nothing beats word-of-mouth advertising. Beware: This rule goes both ways. Don't let your reputation precede you in a negative light.
- The world runs on personal connections. Whether you're referred by a former client to their friend, referred by an alumnus on a college application, or referred by a current employee on a job application, the odds will almost always be on your side when you have a personal connection. Meet people, grow your network, and always stay in touch.
- Know the true value of every experience. While many experiences in school and early in your

career may not pay a lot, the opportunity cost usually makes up for it. Take advantage of these opportunities as ways to learn, grow your skills, and broaden your professional network.

Chapter 4:
Skill Building Doesn't End with Functional Skills

While DJing, running my own business, and providing production support for events was fun, it was never my long-term plan. I may have quit singing and acting on stage in fifth grade, but no matter what those girls said or did to me, they didn't have an ounce of impact on my love for theatre and the arts. I continued to stay involved with theatre throughout middle school and with my new-found interest in audio and production work and my technology know-how, I naturally found that technical theatre was an amazing fit for me, much more so than being on stage. I can't say that I did much in the world of technical theatre in my middle school years as I was limited to four wired microphones, two speakers, and fluorescent lights in a school cafeteria, but by the time I got to high school, the ball started rolling quickly.

The year before entering high school, I got involved with activities like marching band and drama club. It was my goal to meet as many of the current students and staff at the high school as I could in order to hit the ground running once I started as a freshman. Even as a fourteen-year-old, I played to the power of networking.

 Director's Note:
Networking doesn't have an age restriction. The best time to start building your professional network was yesterday. The second-best time is today. Networking can be as simple as taking the time to get to know your teachers, professors, or coworkers. Ask them about their careers, interests, and what led them to where they are. When the question comes up, share your career goals. You never know who they may know or the relevant experience they may have to share.

A few months before high school started, there was an open house for all of the local eighth graders who would be starting as freshmen the following September where each of the school activities had an information booth set up to advertise their club. Going into that night, I had two goals in mind: 1) meet the people from the school's television station *RVTV,* and 2) find my friends from the drama club. As I walked around the packed cafeteria with my parents, I remember being amazed at the sheer number of clubs and activities.

There was row after row of booths packed with students, teachers, parents, incoming students huddled around tables, and posters plastered with photos, awards, and information. After walking around for a while, I finally came across a table sitting in the corner of the cafeteria. The table didn't have a crowd, a poster, or any fun, eye-catching materials to show off. At the table sat a teacher with a single camera in hand and a small white sheet of paper at the edge of the table that read "RVTV".

Looking back, I have no idea what was said during the conversation. I just remember walking up to the teacher to introduce myself. He shook my hand and said, "Hey, how's it going? I'm Nick," followed by quick word stumble, "I mean, Mr. Marms." I'm sure I expressed my interest in joining RVTV, the school's TV station and television media club, and complimented him on all of the great things I heard about the club, but ultimately all that matters for the sake of this story is that conversation happened over thirteen years ago. Since then, Nick has been my teacher, my coworker, my contractor, my friend, and, most of all, my mentor. He's also the same teacher who helped me land my first internship with CBS Radio.

Years before those initial career-changing conversation with Frank and Gene, I had a very similar situation my freshman year of high school. The first few weeks of freshman year, I was spending most of my free time with RVTV. I was having an awesome time working on the morning news and learning more about shooting and editing than ever before, but it was still my ultimate goal to get into the musical theatre program to work on tech for the shows.

The performing arts center was under renovation, so I wasn't able to get into the theatre for the first few weeks of school. Luckily, I already knew a couple people who were involved in the musical theatre program from my time onstage in middle school. A few weeks into school, I reached out to my friends in the program and asked them who I needed to speak to in order to get involved. They introduced me to the musical theatre and choir director, Ms. V.

Ms. V was known as the best in the community. Her reputation as an extremely tough, thorough, and perfectionist director preceded her, but no one could speak highly enough about her unbelievable talent. Having heard her name throughout grade school, I was both excited and nervous to meet her.

One night as marching band practice was ending, I was walking through the band room to put my trumpet back in the locker. Originally designed to be a scene shop, the band room was a large space just offstage right of the theatre with large doors connected to the stage right wing. The tall sets doors were propped open that night and as I walked through the band room, I was able to peer onto the stage where rehearsal was going on. Ms. V spotted me. Having only met her once, I was surprised she recognized me. She walked over and asked if I was still interested in working on the show. She explained that the show that they were rehearsing was *The King & I*, it opened in a week, and they needed an audio technician. Without asking any questions I immediately replied, "Yes!"

Blocking Note:

Looking back, it probably would have been smart to at least ask when the show was, what the time commitment would be, and what audio equipment I needed to know how to use ... but to this day I typically just go for things and figure them out as I go.

She asked if I had a few minutes to meet the technical director then led me up to the tech booth in the back of the theatre. As I walked up the steps, I saw a skinny guy with a black t-shirt and baseball cap propped up on a stool leaning over the audio console.

Ms. V introduced me, "This is Brett. He's a freshman with a background in technical theatre."

My heart raced a bit out of nervousness, thankful for the reassuring compliment but concerned about whether I could live up to the expectation.

The guy spun around on the stool and reached out for a handshake, "Hi, I'm Paul."

It may not have seemed like it at the time, but this was the conversation that set my career in technical theatre and theme parks in motion.

***

My school's theatre was only a few years old when I started high school. The school had an old auditorium, appropriately called "The Old Auditorium", that had been there since the school opened in the 1930s and while it had some amazing beauty from the era in which it was built, it was small, the technology was out-of-date, and its abilities were very limited. The new theatre was called the PAC, short for Performing Arts Center. It was a fairly large building that housed the main theatre along with the backstage areas, band rooms, visual arts, and scene shop.

While it was a stunningly beautiful facility for a high school, it also had some extreme limitations due to budget cuts. The original plans for the mainstage theatre included balcony seating and a higher ceiling. When the balcony was cut, the height of the roof was lowered and there was no longer enough room for a fly well above the stage. This led to the installation of a winch system instead of a fly rail. Its only real capabilities were to lower the lights and curtains down to the deck for maintenance with little to no ability to fly set pieces.

While these limitations along with interesting facility decisions (such as the utilization of rooms for unintended purposes) put a strain on the theatre's abilities, the theatre's lighting system was a perfect system to learn on, and the audio system had just been upgraded to one of the most advanced audio systems outside of the city. The summer before I started high school, a grant was approved to install a quarter-million-dollar audio system in the main theatre. The system was a state-of-the-art Yamaha digital audio system with an M7CL audio console that had just been released the year before. This was an instance of being in the right place at the right time.

The night I met Paul, the audio console had just finished getting installed. There was literally still plastic on most of the faders. In my first few weeks working in the theatre, I had the opportunity to learn the console directly from Yamaha professionals who were working to punch and tune the system. This was well beyond the average crash course. Just three weeks after the system was installed, I got to put it through its paces while running thirty channels of audio for a production of *The King and I.* While there were still kinks in the systems and the new digital processing technology had a few bugs, I had the Yamaha professional standing right behind me while I mixed the opening weekend of the show. I had no idea at the time, but looking back, most fourteen-year-olds don't get this type of learning opportunity. Heck, many professionals ever get this type of learning opportunity.

Blocking Note:

As you probably have already guessed, yes, I networked with the Yamaha Representative and continued to stay in touch with him over the years. I have since run into him at multiple conventions and have included him in RFP (request for proposal) blasts for half a dozen audio projects. Little did he know networking with a freshman in high school would land him contracts over a decade later. NETWORK, NETWORK, NETWORK!

Dírector's Note:

Take advantage of every learning opportunity that comes your way. There is nothing more valuable than good old knowledge and experience. You never know where your newly learned skills or experience may lead you.

By the end of my freshman year, I knew that console inside and out. That expertise continued to pay off the four following years. When a concert would come in at Six Flags that had the M7CL on their rider, I would get assigned to work the concert so that we had a tech onsite who knew the console. When I was interviewing at theatres and arenas in

Philadelphia, on four separate occurrences the interviewer asked about my level of expertise on the M7CL as it was listed on my resume and that was the console their venues had at the time. Finally, in college when I was interviewing with the Philadelphia Eagles, one of the very first conversations I had with my future boss was about the M7CL and my thoughts on it.

So, you may be thinking, *that's great you were in the right place at the right time but that's not always going to be the case.* That is completely true. There have been plenty of times in my career when I was in the right place at the right time and plenty when I wasn't. For those times when I was though, being in the right place at the right time isn't going to do you any good unless you are able to identify the opportunity and appropriately act on it.

I could have just taken the information the Yamaha professionals were giving me and completely ignored it, but I didn't. I listened intently and wasn't afraid to ask questions. After taking the lessons from the instructors, I could have stopped there and just continued to mix the audio for my high school's shows, not bothering to grow my skills or learn more, but I didn't. Even after the professionals left and the system was fully installed and tuned, I watched instructional YouTube videos (there weren't many in 2007), called Yamaha when I had questions, and spent hundreds of hours playing with that console over the following years to truly master it. Finally, I could have just used my new audio technology skills to just mix at my high school and never bothered to monetize my skills, but I didn't. I listed the M7CL and the Yamaha Digital Audio Processing system on my resume, website, and portfolio and even spoke about it in many of my cover letters when applying to venues I knew used similar systems. These steps along with basic professional networking led to me getting hired to mix audio for dozens of theatres, venues, and events around the Delaware Valley before I graduated high school.

Director's Note:
Learn to identify your marketable skills and take advantage of them. Most skills are marketable. You just have to figure out who needs those skills and is willing to pay for them. When you have a skill you are passionate about growing and you have fun doing it, take advantage of it. Research the market. See who your competition is, who they're working for, and what they're charging.

Example 1: If you are really good at software development and you have fun doing it but you're still in school or have a full-time job that conflicts with your ability to take on an additional job, offer your skills as a freelancer online. There are dozens of platforms for freelancers to advertise their services. Write a description of your skills and interests related to software development, share samples of your work, share your hourly rate, then start placing bids on freelance jobs. (Also, if you're a software developer right now or thinking about getting into it, keep in mind that it is one of the most highly sought-after skill sets on the planet and the average software developer's hourly rate has begun to surpass even the highest paid surgeons. Highly recommend!)

Example 2: If you are really good at baking and you would like to make some money on the side with your skills, but you don't have the means to mass produce or sell your baked goods, teach others. Take your pick. There are dozens of outlets thanks to the internet. You can start a YouTube channel with step-by-step videos of you baking and get paid from the advertising revenue.

You can create a course and sell it on Teachable. You can host live baking sessions on Zoom or Google Hangouts and charge people to join the call. The possibilities are endless, and no matter what you choose, please send me the information—or, better yet, mail me some samples, especially if it's chocolate!

***

My freshman year in the Performing Arts Center at my high school ultimately set my career in technical theatre and production in motion. After the production of *The King and I*, Paul was hired full-time as the technical director for the theatre. Paul and I hit it off immediately. He spent months teaching me about all of the technologies in the theatre, from lighting design and programming to rigging and special effects. We would spend months brainstorming ideas for how to incorporate new technology into shows. He would purposely incorporate technology that we didn't own and hadn't used before into the designs just so we could rent the technology and learn how to use it. His passion for the creative use of technology in the theatre was contagious, and his patient, relaxed personality made him an excellent teacher. Looking back now, it's amazing at only twenty-three, he was one of the best teachers I ever had.

That school year we designed, installed, and ran three mainstage shows, about a dozen concerts and musical events, and ran audio and lighting for dozens of school and community events. By the end of that year, I knew that theatre like the back of my hand and, thanks to Paul, I was years ahead in my knowledge of theatrical technology compared to most students my age.

As spring rolled around, Paul's schedule started to book up, and I was left to run many of the events myself. Little did I know at the time that this was a test. As the end of the school year approached, Paul mentioned that he was very impressed and appreciative of all of the work that I had done and how much my skills had grown that year. He asked if I would be interested in working on his team as a technician at Six Flags that summer.

My eyes lit up with excitement. My friends and I had been season pass holders in years prior, and I spent most of my summers there. While I had never considered working in a theme park, Paul had mentioned that his department was in charge of all of the audio and lighting for the park's shows and concerts. That summer the park was slated to run five daily operational shows, along with a few dozen mainstage concerts and a debut of a nighttime glow parade. He said his team was going to be very busy and he needed plenty of skilled help, especially in lighting.

This was the first time it dawned on me that a theme park would be a fantastic place to work if I wanted to maximize my experience working on shows with as little downtime as possible. Up until that point, I was only working on a few shows per year and months would go by when my audio mixing and lighting programming skills would start to get rusty. Working at a theme park that ran shows daily from April through November was exactly what I needed to keep up my current skills and grow new ones.

It took some work to figure out the logistics of exactly how his team would be able to employ me legally and abide by all of the child labor laws, but just as planned, that summer I joined Paul's team as an AV technician.

I started work just a few weeks before the park opened for the season. I would spend the day in school, work about an hour in the PAC, then catch a ride with Paul to the theme park. Evenings pre-opening were a whirlwind. Most of the performers and staff had school or day jobs as well, so rehearsals wouldn't start until 6 p.m. and it would be dark and cold by 7:30 p.m. We tried to cram in as much rehearsal time on the outdoor stages as we could before it got too cold, then we would move inside to the rehearsal spaces for the last hour or two of the night.

Throughout the entire rehearsal process, I could not contain my excitement. This was my first experience working professional rehearsals, not to mention rehearsing many shows at the same time in the middle of an empty theme park. I will never forget the first night I attended the welcome show rehearsal. We were a week and a half out from opening for the season. The main entrance of the park was packed with performers, choreographers, technicians, directors, and all of the executive staff. The music was blaring, the lights were flashing, and everyone looked like they were having such a great time. I was so inexperienced and naive at the time though that I had no idea how much pressure everyone was under. Looking back, I can't imagine how annoying it must have been for the staff to have me on the crew, this overzealous, incredibly excited, completely green new guy who couldn't keep his mouth shut.

 DÍRECTOR'S NOTE:
It is great to be energetic and excited to jump in and try it all but learn to read the room. There are times to ask questions, offer help, or give your input, and there are times when you should just listen and observe while trying to keep out of the way. This is an incredibly hard lesson to learn and, trust me, I'm still not great at reading a room. I can't begin to list the number of times I was pulled off to the side in my early career and told I needed to chill or keep my mouth shut. It's not that I was wrong to ask questions or offer help. I simply wasn't paying attention to my surroundings and waiting for the appropriate moment to speak up.

As opening day approached, Paul had me programming the lighting for the Looney Tunes show and trained me on how to use the various park audio systems. I didn't really understand what I was supposed to be doing from day to day, but I was having a blast. This is where things got interesting.

Up to this point in my career I was primarily working in schools and community theatres or for my cousin's DJ company. In almost every setting I had worked in, there was flexibility in the way that the operation ran, and I had the ability to question why things were the way they were. Now in a theme park, I was working for a big business where all of the operations ran on standard operating procedures. Procedures were designed and put in place in order to allow the operation to run consistently and smoothly every day at scale. Unfortunately, no one ever explained that to me, which led to me consistently making waves and getting into trouble when I would try to be creative.

These are life lessons that most people aren't formally taught. Most of us grow up being praised for our creativity and our willingness to lend a hand. Unfortunately, in the real world, those things don't always result in praise. Each company and team I have worked for has had a very different culture. Each time I join a new team, it takes me quite some time to really understand how the team functions and what boundaries are in place. Most of this is learning to read a room. Some may call it self-awareness; others may simply call it people skills. I think it's a combination of the two coupled with an understanding of a company culture.

I have been on teams where I have been thrown right in and am expected to lead from day one. Usually these teams are for events or shows where I am being hired as a crew lead or technical director so they are legitimately hiring me to lead the team and share my expertise. In these situations, I've had to speak up and be creative right off the bat to effectively do my job and that is appropriate.

There are other teams I have been a part of where even though I may be the lead or the technical director, the team or company I am working for has a predetermined process that I need to follow, and it is my job to lead the team through that process without the operation flying off the rails. These are the teams that I have always struggled with the most.

While I may not be the most artistic one in the room (I'm seriously no artist at all), I tend to be creative. I love trying new ideas and improving processes. "Because that's how we've always done it" is one of the worst and most damaging phrases spoken in any organization. However, in many cases, there are good reasons why a process or policy has been put in place. When you're the newbie, take time to observe, ask the right questions, and give it some time before you start trying to be creative or make changes. Once you're well-established and people trust you, go for it, ask all the questions, challenge the status quo, and NEVER settle for "because that's how we've always done it."

 Director's Note:
Being new, young, and green is hard, but I promise it gets easier if you're patient and keep on the quieter side in the beginning. Start off by asking questions, learn why things are done the way they are, then give it some time before you start offering input. Once you start to gain trust from those around you and make a name for yourself, by all means, stand up, speak out, question every rule, and NEVER take "this is how we've always done it" as an appropriate answer.

***

Aside from learning a few hard lessons about containing my eagerness and keeping my mouth shut, the summer went relatively smoothly. As a fifteen-year-old having just completed my freshman year of high school, spending the summer working alongside a bunch of recent high school graduates and college students came with a constant awareness of just how different our lives were ... but those are stories for another book.

 ## SHOW NOTES:

- Networking doesn't have an age restriction. The best time to start building your professional network was yesterday. The second-best time is today. Networking can be as simple as taking the time to get to know your teachers, professors, or coworkers. Ask them about their careers and interests and what led them to where they are. When the question comes up, share your career goals. You never know who they may know or the relevant experience they may have to share.

- Take advantage of every learning opportunity that comes your way. There is nothing more valuable than good old knowledge and experience. You never know where your new skills or experience may lead you.

- Learn to identify your marketable skills and take advantage of them. Most skills are marketable. You just have to figure out who needs those skills and is willing to pay for them. When you have a skill you are passionate about growing and you have fun doing it, take advantage of it. Research the market. See who your competition is, who they're working for, and what they're charging.

- It is great to be energetic and excited to jump in and try it all but learn to read the room. There are times to ask questions, offer help, or give your input, and there are times when you should just listen and observe while trying to keep out of the way. This is an incredibly hard lesson to learn and, trust me, I'm still not great at reading a room. I can't begin to list the number of times I was pulled off to the side in my early career and told I needed to chill or keep my mouth shut. It's not that I was wrong to ask questions or offer help. I simply wasn't paying attention to my surroundings and waiting for the appropriate moment to speak up.

- Being new, young, and green is hard, but I promise it gets easier if you're patient and keep on the quieter side in the beginning. Start by asking questions, learn why things are done the way they are, then give it some time before you start offering input. Once you start to gain trust from those around you and make a name for yourself, by all means, stand up, speak out, question every rule, and NEVER take "this is how we've always done it" as an appropriate answer.

Chapter 5:

Burnout (On Stress and Anxiety)

A s I wrote this book, I went through a roller coaster of emotions. While most of them were sheer frustration with the pandemic and working from home, feeling alone in the Bay Area, and just the general uncertainty of 2020 and what the future holds, I strongly believe that not having a primary distraction and having far too much free time played a huge part in that roller coaster as well.

While 2020 was a frustrating year, I did not let my emotions get to me nor did I let them have a negative impact on my work or personal life. At twenty-seven, I have been through enough in my life to have a well-developed map and trusty compass that help me navigate my feelings.

While the coping mechanisms I have developed over the years came easy in retrospect, through the course of writing this book, I reopened old chapters of my life long forgotten. It was wild to look back and realize just how far I came in the last decade and how much better prepared I am to handle these emotions in a healthy way. I took a lot of time to write down stories from my past and compare the state of my emotions during different periods in my life to figure out how I developed emotional intelligence. When comparing my wild, hormonal, roller coaster emotional states from high school to my still wild but very contained (and dare I say calm and controllable) emotional states today, I found one incredibly interesting recurring theme: distractions.

Looking back at my senior year of high school, my SATs were complete, I had been accepted to my number one choice for college, I had about two classes left, and my future was pretty much set. I really had absolutely nothing to be worried about. I had worked my butt off for four years to get to that point, but I could not have been more stressed or anxious. That year was one of the worst years, if not the worst year, of my life.

I was so anxious 24/7 that I would get sick to my stomach completely unexpectedly. I had hives on a weekly basis. I was losing friends left and right because I was miserable to be around, and in my parents' eyes I seemed to be taking a bad turn after everything I had worked so hard to achieve. At the time, I really had no idea what was wrong with me. The stress and anxiety weren't really what I was focused on as much as how sick I was constantly—and I never made the connection between the two. Looking back, it's easy for me to see that I was so stressed and anxious that I was making myself sick, but what the heck was I so stressed and anxious about?

There were a few things that happened my senior year of high school that I can't downplay. A few months before my senior year began, there were a few illnesses in my family that added a lot of mental stress, and it was hard to escape. In December of the same year, one of my best friends and technical theatre mentors was killed in a car accident after being hit by someone with a suspended license who was driving under the influence. I had just spoken to him the night before the accident about how it had been a while since we had seen each other, and we were looking forward to catching up before the theme park season started. The morning after that conversation I received a call from an ex-girlfriend I hadn't heard from in almost four years. She was such a mess, I could barely make out what she was saying, but I managed to make out, "Paul's dead." I nearly dropped the phone.

The following months were a roller coaster of emotions. I was still pretty sick on a weekly basis, my relationship with my parents was deteriorating due to my acting out, and I was losing motivation to continue running my DJ/production company even though it was thriving. At the same time, I was being invited to parties, a friend of mine asked me to be her date for junior prom, and a few months later I got a girlfriend for the first time in nearly four years.

While the positive times were great distractions, I was navigating a new landscape of emotions that I had never experienced before. I had DJ'd a dozen proms, but I had never attended one as a guest, let alone as an insanely beautiful girl's date. I had "talked" to girls before and gone out on "dates", but I had never really had a serious girlfriend. I had never been invited to parties throughout high school so my parents had never had a reason to lay the ground rules for a curfew and would blow their tops when I got home after midnight. It was the perfect storm.

Up to that point in high school, I had been so busy that I didn't have any free time. From an educational perspective, I was focused on classes, studying for the SATs, building my portfolio, completing college applications, and just trying to stay afloat. Education was only a small part of my life though. Nights and weekends were spent designing lighting for school shows, running audio for local community theatre productions, and running my DJ/production company that had my friends and I working anywhere from four to six events per weekend. That doesn't even include the odd jobs I had like working for Six Flags, theatre companies, and even a moving company one summer (that one was a terrible, terrible, terrible idea ... my back still hurts a decade later). Needless to say, high school was an insanely busy time for me.

Then senior year happened. To this day, I am not sure what caused me to crash like I did senior year. It may have simply been burnout after three years of a nonstop schedule. It may have been the hormones involved in finally getting the attention of girls, or it may have just been a classic case of senioritis. No matter what the culprit was, this was the beginning of the end of the momentum that got me through high school.

Toward the end of that year, one of my teachers recommended that I apply for the KYW Newsradio News Studies program. For those of you not from Philadelphia or South Jersey, KYW is the local CBS news radio station. At that point in the year, I was looking for anything to keep me busy. All of my school's shows were complete for the year, the few classes I had remaining before graduation were all electives, and I wanted to start gaining experience outside of technical theatre.

I grew up loving the radio. There was a local station I would listen to religiously as a kid, WPST, whose nighttime host was the son of one of my middle school teachers. Although everyone I knew who worked in radio told me to find anything to do for a living other than working in radio, I figured taking a six-week news studies course with the most well-known Newsradio station in the Delaware Valley couldn't hurt my young resume.

The course was a series of workshops that took place on Saturday mornings in Old City, Philadelphia. It was the most exciting and freeing feeling to drive myself into the city every Saturday morning knowing that my parents completely approved and there wasn't any risk of an argument when I returned home. The workshops were pretty interesting. Each session usually started with a guest speaker from the local media industry who would speak about their fulfilling career in radio and television and share a few crazy stories from their years in journalism. I will never forget the journalist who spoke to us during the third week's session about his experience reporting on the MOVE bombing in Philadelphia in 1985. Speaking to a room of high schoolers, he described the dark details of that day, including taking shelter under a car when the bomb was dropped. He played back the audio recording he had from that day, and you could hear a pin drop as the room went silent.

After the guest speaker was finished presenting, we would break into smaller groups with designated reporters who would lead work sessions targeted in different areas of broadcast journalism. While I was never much into journalism, I loved these sessions because the reporter who ran our group was a reporter I had grown up listening to on the radio. It was so cool to be sitting there listening to him teach our class. At times I would close my eyes and just listen, imagining that I was sitting in the back seat of my parent's car on my way to kindergarten listening to KYW on the radio. Then I would open my eyes and there he was, reporting to us right at the front of the room. Even though I never intended to be on the radio, it was a thrilling experience to get a peek behind the scenes of a broadcast that I had listened to almost every day of my childhood.

The final project for the program was for each student to work with their designated reporter to develop a one-minute news report. In the final week of the program, we would record our report in the KYW studios to be broadcast at a later date. As the program came to an end, they announced that there would be awards for the top news reports. The news reports would be rated in different categories and there would be various awards for each category consisting of different scholarships. The top award was a paid internship in the KYW Newsradio studios. As soon as I heard about this opportunity, I knew I had to go for it. In order to qualify for the internship, those who were interested had to apply ahead of time and interview with the news director. Whether I landed the internship or not, I knew just getting to interview would be a fantastic experience.

During the weeks leading up to the end of the program and the internship interview, I felt more normal than I had all year. My stress levels were down. I was less anxious. I was excited to get up early every Saturday and drive into the city for the program, and I was focused on my new goal: landing the internship. It was an amazing to feel like myself again, and ultimately it paid off when I nailed the interview.

The awards ceremony was held a few weeks after the program ended in the atrium at the Franklin Institute in Philadelphia. This in itself was an incredibly special opportunity for me. I grew up going to the Franklin Institute and that played a key part in my love of science and technology. Getting to attend an awards ceremony there was a dream come true—a dream I never even knew I had.

I remember that night like it was yesterday. My mom was having a really tough week and wasn't sure she was going to be able to make the drive into the city with us. Luckily, fighter that she was, she made the trip. My dad drove us into the city and we parked in the garage attached to the museum. As we headed up the elevator into the museum's lobby, we discussed how none of us had ever been to the museum after hours. We had been members of the museum for years, attended countless shows and exhibits, and any time friends and family visited from out of town we would be sure to take them there. All of this history but never once had we attended a private event there.

When we arrived in the lobby, we checked in and were told to take our seats. In typical graduation form, I was sitting with the other graduating students of the News Studies program class while my parents were in the guest section a few rows back. As I sat and waited for the program to begin, I couldn't help but stare up at the cathedral-style dome ceiling. It was a massive room that I had walked through dozens of times before, but its beauty and sheer size never ceased to impress me. In the center of the room was a giant sculpture of Ben Franklin seated in a chair, similar to the sculpture in the Lincoln Memorial.

The program started with the program director welcoming everybody and thanking students for their participation in the news studies program. She then welcomed the guest speaker to the stage, Larry Kane, an American Journalist who spent thirty-six years as a news anchor in Philadelphia having worked for all three major television networks. My parents both had lived their whole lives in or near Philadelphia, and they were in awe of the talent in the room. Having Kane as a speaker had a powerful impact on the evening, reminding everyone in the room of Philadelphia's deep history in broadcast journalism and what it meant to be a part of a program like the one all of us were graduating from that night.

As Kane's speech ended, the program moved on to calling the graduates to the stage to collect their certificates and take photos. Once all of the graduates had crossed the stage and were back in their seats, the news director took the stage again to announce the outstanding news reports that were nominated for awards. As I listened to all of the award winners getting announced, I remember clearly thinking that there was no way that my report could shake a stick at most of theirs. After all, I had never been much into writing or journalism. I was much more interested in being a tech guy behind the scenes.

The news director announced the final award, congratulated all of the recipients, then moved on to talk about the internship opportunity. Out of 200 students in the program, a few dozen applied and interviewed for the position. She gave a brief history of the program along with the back story of how the internship received its name, the *Mark Drucker Internship.*

She thanked all of the applicants who took the time to apply and interview and announced that there were two students who they had selected for the internship. My heart started to race. Up until that point in the evening, I was completely calm. I genuinely didn't think I had a chance of winning any of the awards for the best news story, and I wasn't surprised when they made it through the list without my name being called. I felt much differently about the internship. Although I was just another eighteen-year-old high school student, just like all 200 other students in the program, I was confident that my experience stood out. I had four years of DJ experience, including founding and operating my own company, I had worked in technical entertainment for Six Flags, and I had references listed on my resume that included everyone from my high school superintendent to my Rabbi.

As she led up to announcing the first name, I could feel my palms starting to sweat.

"Emily Schwinn," a name that was not mine sounded confidently through the PA system, followed by a loud cheer from the crowd.

My eyes were laser-focused on the stage, watching the news director's lips get ready to call the second name.

"And the second student awarded the 2011 KYW News Studies Mark Drucker Internship, Brett Axler."

My heart beat out of my chest and I could barely breathe as I confirmed I had actually just heard my name called. Above the polite applause from the crowd there was a clear shriek of delight that came from a few rows behind me and echoed through the atrium's dome ceilings. I didn't even have to turn around before I was smiling ear-to-ear recognizing that shriek as my mom's.

That night stands fresh in my memory to this day. In the weeks leading up to the interview and then the wait leading up to that night, I had no idea that the pure joy from that night would have next to nothing to do with actually landing the internship and everything to do with brightening up my mom's year by making her proud.

By that point in the year, I had my emotions well in check. I was eager to finish up the school year and graduate, then move on to my summer internship at KYW before starting college in September. I was on cloud nine and I felt like nothing could touch me. Little did I know that all I was doing was suppressing my real emotions and slowly building up pressure that would lead to an inevitable explosion.

Out of some act of a higher power, and some of the most amazing friends and mentors I still have to this day (*thank you, Nick, Bill, Kristine, and Deb*), I made it safely through the rest of senior year and started the internship with KYW just after graduation. That summer was an interesting one from the start because it was the first summer in four years that I did not have a full-time job. KYW had me on the evening shift in the newsroom a few nights a week to start the summer before moving to the third shift on the weekends once my training was complete. Other than that, I did not have any work lined up and DJing was pretty slow during the summers. I felt lucky to have a girlfriend and friends in town who were also free most of the summer and figured that would keep me fairly busy and out of trouble.

As training in the newsroom began, I was fully focused on learning as much as I could and proving to the team that I was there with open ears. My primary job was a production assistant. The day shifts had me occasionally moving the anchors' cars or filling their parking meters, getting coffee, and making copies—standard PA work. Although most of it was mindless work, I really didn't mind it because I just loved being part of the operation and I thought it was the coolest thing to have a badge I had to scan to get in the front door of the building and be granted access to all of the CBS-operated floors in the tower. At the time, the studios were located on 400 Market Street in Philadelphia along with many of the other CBS stations. On the occasional morning shift I would find myself in the elevator with Danny Bonaduce from the seventies TV show *The Partridge Family* and various sports reporters I had spent my entire life listening to and watching on TV.

The evening shifts were a little less exciting. The shifts would start at the closing bell of the stock market, so I'd spend the first hour working with finance reporters supporting them on their closing bell market reports. Once their show was over, they would leave along with most of the day shift folks and I would be left to answer the phones and prepare the weather reports for the next few hours until the overnight shift anchors came in.

There were hours that would pass when I had absolutely nothing to do. If the Phillies were in town for a home game, the whole sports center would be broadcasting from the stadium, so it would just be an engineer and I manning the studio. When the Phillies were away, the studio was a little livelier and I would get to shadow the guys. I remember sitting and watching the game on the studio monitors thinking how much fun it would be to work in the control room at the games. If I only knew that just a year later, that's exactly what I would be doing.

While training in the newsroom progressed and I was assigned to more shifts, life with my friends and family started to fall by the way-side again. Things were getting weird between me and my girlfriend. I started to have a hunch that the guy she was "just friends" with was a little more than that, and our mutual friends started to be really secretive about what they were all up to while I was at work. There were a number of parties my friends hosted that I wasn't invited to, and when I confronted them about it the excuse was typically, "No man, we thought you were working and we didn't want you to feel left out, so we didn't tell you about it." They said all that while proceeding to upload photos of the party on Facebook. All of this was starting to weigh on me and the anxiety of feeling left out and wondering what my girlfriend was actually up to was starting to crack my facade of happiness.

As slow evening shifts turned into dead third shifts, I started to run out of activities to keep me occupied. The worst were the Friday–Sunday third shifts when I would arrive at work around 9 p.m. just as all of my friends were going out to enjoy their weekends. The first few hours of the shift I would remain fairly busy filing all of the tapes from the day's broadcast and preparing the newsroom for overnight automation. Once the clock hit midnight, the evening anchors left and it was just me and my thoughts for four incredibly long hours. It was like being Chris Pratt in the 2016 movie *Passengers*. My only tasks were to answer the phones and make sure that the automated systems kept the replays of news and weather reports running.

Those were the first of many overnight shifts I've since worked in my professional career. I've spent nights sitting in show barges out in the middle of lakes in Disney World being a glorified babysitter for design contractors. I've spent nights checking for leaks in entertainment electrical rooms while hunkered down in the middle of a hurricane. I've even spent nights on the rooftops of the Magic Kingdom manually replacing over 2,500 firework pins in 99 percent humidity, and I can still say without a doubt that those overnight shifts working by myself in the newsroom at KYW were the worst overnight shifts of my life. Now this is not a slight on my former employer or even the situation I was in. The fact that I was alone with next to nothing to do is also not something I blame. The only person I have to blame for my perceived torture is myself.

While most of the overnights I've worked in years since I have been accompanied by coworkers and actually have work to do, I have spent quite a few overnights alone with nothing to do, without air conditioning, being eaten by mosquitoes and listening to the BGM loops of *It's A Small World* on replay that haven't been half as bad as those nights alone in the newsroom. Why is this?

Perception.

While I sat in that cushy, air-conditioned newsroom for all of those overnights, with the world at my fingertips, I decided to spend my time stressing about what my *perceived* friends were doing without me and visualizing my girlfriend cheating on me with her "just friend." In reality, I was being paid to sit in a perfectly safe, uninterrupted environment, with internet access and state-of-the-art studios that I had permission to practice in.

Where do I even begin on the mistakes and lessons learned here?!

First off, let's get the obvious out of the way. If you have reason to believe that you are being cheated on and your significant other, along with all of your friends, is being abnormally secretive and clearly hiding something from you, they probably are. Nip that situation in the butt and get on with your life. They're not worth your time and definitely not worth you potentially ruining your career over.

Next, your situation is completely controllable based on perspective. Twenty-seven-year-old me wants to go back to eighteen-year-old me and slap him across the face right as his head begins to hit the desk dozing off on one of those overnight shifts. I could have been learning how to use the studios, watching the available tutorials, practicing my radio voice, building a demo reel … need I go on? Instead, I was refreshing Facebook, torturing myself with stress and anxiety over friends who weren't actually my friends and a girlfriend who surprise, surprise, ended up dating her *just a friend* mere weeks after we broke up. I haven't spoken to any of them in almost ten years and they hadn't even crossed my mind once until I started writing this chapter.

Director's Note:
They're not worth your time. There are seven billion people on this planet. Stop wasting time, stress, and energy fighting for friends or significant others who aren't worth fighting for. You'll know when you've found ones worth keeping around.

Do you have time to kill stuck at home or working third shifts in a place less exciting than a newsroom? There are these incredibly rare things that you can use to pass time that far too many people have never heard of (including eighteen-year-old me): books. Read a book, watch a class, check out *YouTube Learning,* take free online certification courses from the country's top universities. I can go on endlessly with more ideas for how to make the time pass while being productive and learning something new and valuable. Even as I am writing this, I am using this chapter as a way to pass time and practice a new skill while stuck at home during the COVID-19 pandemic.

Thank you for coming to my TED Talk.

Director's Note:
Use your time and resources wisely. With the world at your fingertips, it's easy to be distracted by big time wasters. Flipping through social media is not only a huge waste of time but it's proven to drag your mood and motivation down as well. Delete social media from your phone or add strict time limits. Use the time to grow your skills or learn something new. You can not only learn endless new skills online but can earn accredited certifications to boost your resume as well.

Anyway, back to my story. I promised you an explosion, so here it is. As the summer went on, I broke up with my girlfriend, cut all ties with that group of friends, and threw myself into work. Unfortunately, throwing myself into work was just working more long, boring, overnight shifts with nothing to do. As my boredom grew, my stress and anxiety began to creep back into my daily life. I started getting panic attacks while sitting at the desk doing absolutely nothing, my claustrophobia started to spark back up causing anxiety about taking elevators (totally not a great thing when working on the tenth floor), and eventually I wasn't sleeping between shifts, which lead to twenty-four-hour periods of being awake and almost falling asleep at the wheel multiple times on my way home. And it gets worse.

One morning I woke up not able to get out of bed. My back felt like I had a knife in it. (No, this is not a metaphor for my friends and ex-girlfriend). It was this incredibly sharp pain just off the right side of my spine next to my shoulder blade and any direction I rolled felt like a knife was physically being twisted and turned deep into my back. I had to call my mom for help to get out of bed. As I basically crawled over to the bathroom, my mom lifted up the back of my shirt to check my back. In the area I was feeling the pain, she found a small colony of what looked to be pimples. Not making any sense of it, I went right to the doctor and he diagnosed me with shingles—stress-induced shingles, as an eighteen-year-old.

Just as the doctor warned me, the shingles got much worse before they got better. I was down and out for almost three weeks, most days unable to get out of bed or off the couch. The recovery was so slow that I was cutting it close to freshman year orientation and I wasn't sure I was going to be allowed to attend.

This was my breaking point. The bomb had been dropped and now I was experiencing the fallout. I quit the KYW internship, I was stuck at home sick as a dog, and I wasn't even sure I was going to be able to attend my freshman orientation for college. All of my years of hard work, networking, growing my business, and dreaming of my next big step into college all came to a crashing halt and I could only blame myself.

Once I finally physically started to feel better, I began the clean-up and started rebuilding. I started to see a therapist about my stress and anxiety. I allowed myself to be lazy for the first time and just sat home watching movies. Best of all, I started taking frequent trips to spend time with my grandparents. I wasn't able to see it at the time, but this was exactly the type of event that needed to happen in my life to force me to calm down and take time to reevaluate everything that I was taking on.

Up to this point in the book, I have harped on saying yes and taking on as many new experiences as possible. However, as much as some of us wish that we had the ability to work 24/7 without consequence, that is absolutely not the case. We all have a breaking point. Where that point is and what it looks like when you surpass it looks different for everyone but I promise when it shows its nasty face, you won't easily forget it. This is called burnout.

Many of you reading this have probably already experienced burnout and may have an idea of what it looks like when it comes knocking. For those of you fortunate enough not to experience it yet, either you haven't been to college or you live in California or Colorado. There's nothing that will take you down harder than burnout. Whether it's exhaustion that causes you to get into an accident, unhealthy habits or lack of sleep that make you sick, or stress that makes you miserable to be around, it's not a fun experience for you or those around you.

Learning to identify the early signs of burnout comes naturally over time. Admitting to yourself that you're showing signs and actually taking the precautionary steps to do something about it before it explodes requires self-discipline. I've found that unfortunately it's not always the same warning signs, which is what took me so many years and multiple burnouts to make it to where I am today: capable of setting limits for myself and having a mitigation plan in place that I act on at the first sign of burnout.

How you avoid or handle burnout may look slightly different than it does for me but here are a few signs I look out for and the steps I take to avoid an explosion.

Signs of Oncoming Burnout:
- Lower than normal energy levels
- Exhaustion
- Easily irritable
- Inability to concentrate
- Abnormal laziness
- More easily distracted than usual

- A strong change in appetite
- Frequent feeling of emptiness
- Sudden lack of care

Precautionary Steps:
- Immediately prioritize upcoming work
  - High Priority: Get it done ASAP
  - Medium Priority: Schedule a time to get it done then forget about it until then
  - Low Priority: Ask for help, hire someone else, or consider dropping it completely
- Reach out to your boss, coworkers, or professors to let them know you are feeling overextended and ask if they can help deprioritize some of your work
- Cancel or postpone all unnecessary activities and plans
- Say "no" or "not now" to anything that's not critical
- Turn off the TV and get some sleep
- Work with your boss to plan time off as soon as possible
- Go buy as much Ben & Jerry's ice cream as your cart can fit

 SHOW NOTES:
- They're not worth your time. There are seven billion people on this planet. Stop wasting time, stress, and energy fighting for friends or significant others who aren't worth fighting for. You'll know when you've found ones worth keeping around.
- Use your time and resources wisely. With the world at your fingertips, it's easy to be distracted by big time wasters. Flipping through social media is not only a huge waste of time but it's proven to drag your mood and motivation down as well.

Delete social media from your phone or add strict time limits. Use the time to grow your skills or learn something new. You can not only learn endless new skills online but can earn accredited certifications to boost your resume as well.

- Learn to recognize the signs of oncoming burnout and act quickly. Don't try to be a hero. Everyone needs a break at some point. You won't be help to anyone, especially yourself, once you've past the point of burnout.
- There's no shame in saying no, asking for help, or seeing a therapist. It is perfectly acceptable to admit to yourself that you can't do it all on your own.

Chapter 6:

Lights, Camera, Football?
(On Discovering Opportunities
You Never Knew Existed)

After a summer of rest, I was ready to hit the ground running as a college freshman. Attending a university that ran on the quarter system meant that school didn't start until late September, each term was only ten weeks, and by week four we were already preparing for midterms. Luckily my high school ran on a similar schedule, so I was prepared for the intense speed of the curriculum.

The first few weeks of freshman year weren't anything to write home about. After four years of intense work and running a business on top of being a full-time student and hormonal teenager, having nothing to do outside of studying for five classes left me with a lot of free time to act my age for once. I got involved in a few activities around campus, made friends with some of the people in my dorm, and almost immediately started creating mischief with my roommates.

My roommates and I lived in one of the newer halls on campus. The dorms were suite style, each with two bedrooms, a bathroom, and a common area, four students to a unit. The units were staggered between guys and girls with about forty residents per floor. One of my roommates was a friend from high school while the other two were randomly placed with us. From day one we knew it was going to be a wild year.

 Blocking Note:

Now let me set your expectations right there before you let your mind wander too much. Our dorm included a bio-chem engineer, a comp science major, a creative architecture major, and yours truly, a technical entertainment nerd studying entertainment and arts management with a minor in theatre. Trust me, we weren't throwing ragers or inviting over all the girls. No, our version of a wild freshman year was installing enterprise grade servers in our dorm, finding the loopholes in our internet service provider's bandwidth caps, and removing all the furniture from our common area to fit a blow-up swimming pool and using a beer bong to funnel the water from the shower to fill it. Needless to say, we made a name for ourselves pretty quickly.

We had a great time, and I honestly enjoyed taking a break from working so hard to refocus my efforts on making friends and just being a kid. Aside from volunteering on the production crew for the Thanksgiving Day Parade and putting in my required work study hours in the school's theatre, I laid low and didn't work much. I was really enjoying this new way of life until I walked into Wawa one morning to purchase a hoagie and my card was declined.

It was a $5 hoagie. I didn't understand. I figured something had to be wrong with my card, so I pulled out my debit card and gave it a swipe.

Declined. What?! Had I been hacked? I checked my wallet for cash and was instantly overwhelmed by a sinking feeling when I realized I didn't even have a dollar to my name. I left the hoagie on the counter and ran out the front door in embarrassment.

I did not understand what was happening. Since the age of thirteen, I had had a paying job. I never had to think twice about spending money on the little things and I had never asked my parents for money. This was my harsh wake-up call. I no longer owned a business. I didn't have events paying the bills, and I didn't have a paying job. As it turned out, hanging with my roommates on the weekends may have been more fun than DJing five parties but it sure didn't pay the bills.

I jumped right into action and started researching jobs around campus: front desk receptionist at the recreation center, university library assistant, box office clerk at the theatre … all the jobs looked horribly boring and far below my skill level. I ran a business for four years, mixed audio in 5,000-seat arenas, and produced a video for the governor's PR event. There was no way I was going to go from that to checking university ID cards at the front desk of the recreation center. I was going to have to think outside the box.

Now I would assume your first question might be why I didn't just make a few calls and pick up work DJing or running audio for events again. I very well could have picked up a few gigs within a week or two, but that was exactly the life I was trying to avoid going back to. While DJing was fun in high school when the only alternative to working on a Saturday night was hanging at home, being in college in Philadelphia with some 38,000 other college students meant that spending my week-ends DJing weddings and bar mitzvahs was the last thing that I wanted to do. I was eighteen for crying out loud, can you blame me?

One night late in the first semester, a few of my friends talked me into following them to rush night at frat row. This was the night that all the fraternities and sororities held open houses to convince freshmen to rush. I had zero interest in Greek life but I decided to tag along. As we went from house to house, we heard the same spiel over and over as a bunch of upperclassmen pretended to like us and told us about the amazing opportunities their house had to offer.

Aside from rolling my eyes at the poor performances I witnessed that night, I did take the time to network (Of course, you didn't think just because I took a break from work meant that it was time to slack off on professional networking, did you?) At each house, I spoke to the brothers about their events and who they typically hired to DJ. Most of the houses had the same story about how one of their brother's was "the best DJ in Philly." (Sure, bro, because the best DJ in Philly spends his weekends mixing in a dingy frat house basement on West 34th street getting paid in beer.) Either way, I handed my personal business card to at least one of the brothers at each house and told them to give me a call if they ever needed a DJ.

Director's Note:
Get personal business cards created and have them on you at all times. They don't need to be anything fancy. They just need to get the point across. You can go to any printing website and order your first batch of 500 for less than you'll spend at the bar this weekend, and unlike the bar tab, it will be money that will eventually come back to you many times over. By the time I cleaned out my desk drawer at the end of my senior year of college, I had well over 200 business cards collected from various student leaders and local business owners. It doesn't matter if your business card literally just says your name and major on it along with your contact information. The point is to have a tangible card to be able to hand to people when networking. You never know when it may come in handy, but it will pay off.

After that night at frat row, I didn't hold my breath to get a call from anyone. I was more than confident that most, if not all, of the cards I handed out ended up in the trash or the lint filter in one of the dryers at the local laundromat, but that didn't bother me. Even at eighteen, I knew that a single business card cost me less than $.07. Multiply that times the twenty-one cards I handed out that night and, at most, I lost $1.47 along with a few hours of my time. The opportunity cost far outweighed the $1.47 and my effort. All it was going to take was one brother to leave my card sitting on a table somewhere or drop it on his desk and come across it when planning a large event and my effort would have paid for itself one hundred times over, if not more.

***

The best boss I ever had was the last leader I reported to while working for Disney in Orlando. I'll tell you plenty more about what made him such an amazing leader later in the book but for now let me just share a lesson of his:

> "An experienced salesman doesn't let a rejection affect their motivation. A great salesman gets motivated by rejection."

Why in the world would anyone get motivated by rejection? Especially a salesperson who's working on commission and has to feed their family? Statistics. It's a numbers game. A rejection just means that the salesman is one step closer to their next sale. There are over 7.5 billion living people on this planet, and the only thing that every last one of us has in common is a heartbeat. *(Yes, I know there are a few more similarities than that, but give me a break; it's a good quote and I'm trying to make a point here.)*

Simply put, there are a lot of people on this planet, each one very different from the rest. The goal isn't as much to convince the people who aren't interested to be interested as it is to find the people who are already interested. The numbers vary between lines of business and team statistics but the common rule of thumb I've always been taught is that every seventh pitch should lead to a sale.

(Please don't get too hung up on this idea. Again, every business will be different. I can't wait to get the angry emails, although at least that means you formed enough of an opinion of my work to go out of your way and email me!)

Jokes aside, rejection is going to happen to everyone—rejection from a university, rejection from an audition, rejection from a girl (I am very experienced in this type of rejection), rejection from a job (I am much less experienced in this type of rejection, which is in part why I am writing this book). Rejection happens, but that just means you're one step closer to not being rejected. You have 7.49 billion people to go, and there's no time to waste!

***

About two months after that rush night, I was walking out of rehearsal when I got a call from a local phone number. It was a DJ from TKE who said he got my number from one of the fraternity brothers. "Hey man, I'm really in a bind. We've got a social tonight and I've got a dead speaker. Do you have one I can rent?"

Jackpot.

Over the next three years of college until I moved out of Philadelphia, I rented out my DJ, audio, and lighting equipment about sixty-five weekends to an endless list of clients all generated by word of mouth—starting with a single business card that I handed out two months into freshman year at a Greek life rush event.

Put down this book right now and order yourself business cards.

***

While renting out my DJ equipment to local parties definitely generated some consistent income and paid for the equipment a few times over, it was not enough to cover much more than my rent on a monthly basis, so I knew I had to continue looking for work. Aside from avoiding picking up DJ gigs that would keep me out all hours on the weekends, my primary goal was to find a job that I enjoyed and that would continue growing my skills in technical theatre. My career goals at that point were somewhere between working on shows at Disney and designing lighting on Broadway. It honestly changed by the day. Either way I knew the perfect job for me would be working in the tech department for one of the many theatres around Philadelphia. The problem was that most of the theatres in the city were union houses* and I was not a card holder and the few theatres that were not union houses were all very competitive to get into because they were flooded with college students in my same situation.

*Footnote: A union house is a theatre term for a theatre that is under contract with a local labor union, typically IATSE (International Alliance of Stage Employees). Most of the Philadelphia theatres are under contract with IATSE Local 8.

As part of my class requirements during the fall semester of my freshman year, I was assigned to work backstage on a production of *A Midsummer Night's Dream*. This wasn't the first Shakespeare show I had worked on. Having never been a huge fan of Shakespeare or straight plays, I knew what I was getting myself into—or, at least, I thought I knew. This production was not a normal production; this was a Beach

Boys production of *A Midsummer Night's Dream*. As if I didn't believe the show could get any weirder, I was assigned to the flyrail* for a show with a single scene change. Needless to say, it was a less than thrilling experience, but as the freshman on tech crew, I tried to keep a positive attitude. (My former classmates may say my use of "tried" here is being generous, but hey, live and learn.)

> *Footnote: The flyrail in a theatre is the area backstage where all of the rope is anchored to counterweight the hanging set pieces, lights, and hardware on stage. In a standard proscenium style theatre, the flyrail is the place backstage where flymen are staged to control the movement of the set pieces.

During the production, I got to spend a lot of time backstage getting to know the upperclassman on crew. They were a nice group of guys and girls, typical theatre geeks, my kind of crowd. They kept talking about their plans for the upcoming Fringe Festival. I had heard plenty about the Edinburgh Fringe Festival in Scotland that students and faculty from my program attended each year but this was my first time learning anything about a Fringe Festival that took place in Philadelphia. They described it as the busiest weeks of their lives each year when they worked on dozens of shows in theatres around the city and ended every night at a different bar. On top of all that, it paid really well. I just remember thinking, "Sign me up!"

As it turned out, the reason why most of the crew worked the festival was because the technical director of the festival was a contractor who frequently worked in our school's theatre. The first chance I got to talk to him I immediately expressed my interest in working on the festival and asked how I could get involved. He explained that the festival took place the last few weeks of each summer and every year his staffing needs changed. He told me he would likely be able to find a position for me but would not know for sure until the summer got closer so I should follow up with him then. I thanked him for the information and set a reminder on my calendar to reach out to him as the summer approached.

Director's Note:
While remembering to follow up with someone about an opportunity a few months out may be seemingly simple, life gets in the way, things change, and it's easy to forget. Setting a simple reminder on your calendar or sending a scheduled email to yourself to be delivered around the time that you need to be reminded can be a lifesaver. It takes just a few minutes. Make a few notes about the conversation, add the details you need to remember and the contact info of the person you need to talk to, then schedule it and forget about it until the time comes.

As the year went on, I picked up a few small gigs here and there. Toward the end of each month when rent was going to be tight, I would pick up a gig DJing for one of the companies I used to partner with. It was easy money and a great way to keep my foot in the door with the DJ and entertainment community that I had worked to build my name and reputation in for so many years.

Director's Note:
Stay in touch and keep your name relevant.

***

An interesting fact about Drexel University (where I attended) is that their football team hasn't lost a game since 1978. Of course, they haven't played a game since 1978, but hey, the fact remains true! The football team at Drexel is actually the comedy club. The school hasn't had a real football team since the seventies, and the school's biggest sport when I was there was basketball. Since basketball is played primarily in the winter, the school would host homecoming in January instead of October or November like most other schools that plan their homecoming around the football season.

Each year for homecoming, the Drexel DAK PAC, the basketball team's official fan club, would host celebrations around campus and sell out the basketball arena. After the game the celebrations would continue with a student-planned concert hosted in the 33rd Street Armory. The armory is a former military staging warehouse that was turned into an annex for the school's athletic center. As a giant, enclosed building in the center of campus it made for the perfect concert venue for a bunch of crazy college students.

The week leading up to homecoming weekend I started to see the trucks rolling up to the armory to drop off the concert equipment. One morning on my way to class I recognized one of the trucks that was parked outside. Printed on the front driver's door of the truck was "Earl-Girls Rentals." My eyes lit up and I ran inside the armory to find my former coworkers. EarlGirls was the AV company Paul and I used to work with for the events at my high school and Six Flags, among many other events around South Jersey and Atlantic City.

As I entered the venue, I immediately ran into one of my old coworkers, "Dude! How the heck are you? What are you doing at Drexel?!"

We got to talking and, as it turned out, they were contracted by another local AV production company to rent and transport equipment for the concert. He introduced me to the owner of the company in charge, Kevin. We had a quick conversation about the show, the rig they were installing, and of course the crazy asks that were on the show rider. The headliner was Snoop Dogg, so naturally it was a wild rider with all types of crazy asks.

Kevin asked if I planned on attending the concert and I told him it wasn't really my scene having spent years working concerts and events. His eyes lit up, "Oh, what shows have you worked?"

We went on to talk about Six Flags and the shows in Atlantic City before he asked if I wanted to shadow his crew for the weekend. Of course, I said yes, and next thing I knew it was Saturday night and I was rushing back from South Jersey after dropping off equipment for a DJ rental to make it back just in time for Waka Flocka Flame's opening act.

Shadowing the production team for the concert led me to meeting the student board who planned the concert. Meeting the student board led me to joining the student board. Joining the student board led me to assisting with planning the following year's homecoming concert. Planning the following year's homing concert led me to co-leading the student board. Co-leading the student board led to me making a name for myself around campus as the events guy and I was soon hired by the university's Office of Student Affairs to handle the planning of AV contracts and logistics for all the large events on campus. This trend continued for the rest of my time at Drexel. By the end of my senior year, I had produced about a dozen concerts, countless events, and had grown my professional network to include everyone from the Dean of Students to the West Philadelphia Chief of Police.

All of this came from one simple conversation with an old coworker. The coworker was the truck driver for the AV company who used to drop off rental gear to my high school.

 DIRECTOR'S NOTE:
It doesn't matter who you are talking to. Everyone, and I mean everyone, could be the connection to your next big break.

Simple Rules of Engagement:

- Be a nice person
- Treat everyone fairly
- Introduce yourself
- Speak up
- Ask questions
- Stay in touch

***

As freshman year came to an end, I reached out to Derek at the theatre and asked him if he knew what his staffing needs were going to be for the summer Fringe Festival. As it turned out, that summer the Fringe Festival was rebranding itself and preparing to announce their expansion and groundbreaking on a new performance venue. Derek mentioned that it was going to be a busy summer and he was going to need a lot of help around the office. He asked if I would like to be his Assistant Technical Director and without missing a beat I said yes.

That summer was nothing short of insane. From crew scheduling to payroll, technical design reviews to site walks, and load-ins to rehearsals, it was a seven-day-a-week job that kept me on my feet and driving around the city fourteen hours a day to dozens of venues.

I loved every second of it.

This type of schedule wasn't anything new for me. It was very similar to the schedule I managed in high school minus classes since I was on summer break.

Each day I was meeting new professionals, from Broadway directors and designers to local up-and-coming artists. As you might imagine, I was in networking heaven. Best of all I was getting to work in all of the venues I had grown up attending shows in. As I walked into each theatre to meet the crews, drop off equipment, and check in with the show staff,

I would stand in the center of the stage, take a long, slow look around the theatre, and just take a moment to appreciate where I was.

 Blocking Note:

All of my fellow theatre geeks understand the feeling of standing on the edge of the apron of the stage staring out into the audience in awe of the opportunity you have been given. As Neil Patrick Harris so eloquently put it during his 2013 Tony's Opening Number, "There's a kid in the middle of nowhere who's sitting there living for Tony performances. Singing and flipping along with the Pippins, and Wickeds, and Kinkys, Matildas, and Mormons. So, we might reassure that kid, and do something to spur that kid, because I promise you, all of us up here tonight, we were that kid." Anyone crazy enough to work in theatre is doing it because they can't possibly imagine doing anything else. It's not just a job, it's not just art, it's not just performance—it's the passion in our blood that keeps our heart pumping.

As the rest of the summer went on and the Festival's shows began to open, my schedule only continued to get crazier. As much as I was loving the experiences I was having, I started to get an inkling that I was nearing a point of exhaustion. With my senior year of high school only a year behind me, I quickly became nervous about my feelings of burnout resurfacing. I started to think about what I could do to relax a bit. The problem was that all of my interests were in theatre and technology, neither of which would allow me to take my mind off work. This realization was concerning. My passion and all of my interests were directly tied to my everyday work, and there was no escaping it. I needed to either find new interests outside of theatre and entertainment or start to consider career paths that would allow me to take a break from everything I had ever known.

***

One afternoon that summer, my brother gave me a call asking if I wanted to go with him to a Phillies game. As much as I was not a fan of sports, I agreed without hesitation. Taking the evening off and spending it with my brother sounded like a fantastic way to relax and get my mind off the stresses of work.

It was a beautiful summer evening, perfect for baseball. We purchased tickets for a pair of seats in the outfield and relaxed watching the game. While my brother was focused on the game itself, calling out players' names, reading the stats, and being the true sports fan in our row, I couldn't take my eyes off the video board. I had only been to a small handful of baseball and basketball games over the years—never once by choice—and I had never once even stepped foot into a football stadium or seen a hockey game. As I stared at the giant video board shining over left field, I noticed entertainment folks walking around the stadium along with camera operators running trivia contents and handing out prizes to fans between innings. I had never noticed that before. It looked fascinating, like it would be a lot of fun.

I sat thinking about how there were roughly eighty home games per season, most games were on nights and weekends, and the stadium was just a few subway stops away from my dorm. It would be a fantastic job!

During the seventh inning stretch, my brother and I were taking a walk around the outfield concession area when I came across the outfield camera operator platform. I walked up to one of the cameramen and asked him how he liked working the games. He said he loved it, it was a relaxed gig, and it kept him busy after his day job. When I inquired about his day job, he mentioned that he was a camera operator for CBS.

I exclaimed, "No way! I worked as an intern at CBS last summer!"

As it turned out, he worked at the newer studio, so our paths had never crossed. But it definitely helped the conversation to highlight some of our professional similarities. As the inning break ended and he had to get back to work I quickly asked him if he knew who I could talk to about work or internship opportunities working the games. He read off the name and email address of the video producer and told me to reach out to him and let him know that Tim had referred me. I thanked him and headed back to the seats with my brother.

 Director's Note:

Walking up to strangers can be intimidating for most people, I completely understand the feeling. Personally, while I've never been intimidated to meet anyone new in a professional setting, put me in front of a girl at a social event and I'll forget my name. Put me in front of the same girl at a networking event and we'll chat about our careers and aspirations until the night ends. Try to manage this fear and work diligently to get over it. The worst thing that can happen is the person ignores you. The second worst thing is the person blows you off, but that's about it. The best things that can happen are endless. Remember, everyone is a potential connection. Everyone knows somebody that you don't know.

The second I got home that night I sent the producer an email. I introduced myself as a local college student looking for internship opportunities. I explained that I had a background in technical theatre and a decent amount of experience in radio and TV from my time working in my school's television station and interning with CBS. I attached my resume, thanked him for his time, and confidently clicked send.

After about a week of not hearing back, I decided to send a simple follow-up email:

Hi Mr. Edwards,

Hope all is well, just following up to see if you or anyone on the team may have available internship opportunities for an ambitious college student.

Thanks,
Brett Axler

Another week passed by without getting a response. This time I decided that instead of following up again, I would look for other resources.

*** *** ***

A few weeks into my freshman year of college, I was sitting in an intro class for my major when the professor asked the class to raise our hands if we had a LinkedIn profile set up. About half the class raised their hands. The professor responded, "Okay, for those of you who haven't set up a LinkedIn profile yet, you're late to the party. Get it done tonight and connect with me for a review. For those of you who already have profiles set up, I want you to spend the evening researching the profiles of professionals in the positions you are aspiring for and take notes on how you can improve yours to get to their level."

I already had my LinkedIn profile set up from an assignment in one of my high school business classes. I hadn't touched my profile since though, and it didn't even list the college I was attending, let alone any impactful career skills. That night I updated my profile, found a picture that didn't look like I was fifteen years old, and started researching profiles of professionals who I already knew in the technical theatre and live entertainment industry.

Throughout the rest of freshman year, I continued to groom my profile, adding relevant skills, connecting with professors and classmates, and adding information about my work experience. By the end of freshman year, I had a few hundred connections and a fairly well-established profile that I was proud of.

***

After not hearing back from the Phillies producer, I decided to do some research on LinkedIn. I researched the production folks for the Philadelphia sports teams and looked to see if I had any first- or second-degree connections who I could reach out to for advice on landing an internship. After what seemed like just a few minutes of searching, I came across the profile of a young associate producer with the Philadelphia Eagles who I had a second-degree connection with. The connection we had in common was a guy named Rob who I had worked on a few of the concerts with around Philadelphia. I reached out to Rob, explained I was looking for internship opportunities with local sports teams, and asked if he would be willing to introduce me to his connection at the Eagles. Rob did exactly that and within a day I had a response from the associate producer asking me if I was available to come in for an interview the following Friday.

It's been almost a decade since that day, but I can still remember every moment leading up to the interview that Friday. I was so excited I couldn't sleep, and I definitely wasn't able to eat breakfast that morning. None of this was from anxiety though. This was sheer excitement. Working for a sports team had never crossed my mind, and until the moment of my first interview, I had never even been to a football stadium let alone attended a game. I was excited for something new, and I was thrilled by the idea that I had absolutely nothing to lose. Even if the interview went terribly, at least I gave it a try. It wasn't like I was losing out on a lifelong dream. If the interview went great and I got the internship and I hated every second of it because I didn't like sports, then at least it was a great learning opportunity and a pretty neat line to add to my resume and portfolio.

As I entered the NovaCare complex where the interview was being held, I drove through the rows of fancy cars and custom license plates. There were signs above each parking spot highlighting who the spot was reserved for. I couldn't help but think how my dad and brother would be starstruck by the players' and coaches' names. To me, they were just reserved parking spots with fancy cars. I started to get nervous hoping that I wasn't going to get asked any specific questions about the team in the interview. As I approached the building, I started running through names in my head thinking about how many players I could name.

"Well, I know Jeffery Lurie is the owner, Andy Reed is the coach … and Terryl Owans? Is he even a player on this team? I think he plays football. I've heard his name before. Oh, Donavan McNabb. I know his name. Wait, didn't he retire? Oh crap, I'm screwed."

I had dressed up in a suit and tie, just as I had for every other interview. It was the middle of August and training camp was in full swing so there were tons of players, coaches, and staff dressed in sports attire hustling in and of the office buildings. I stuck out like a sore thumb. As I got up to the front door, I called the phone number I was instructed to call when I arrived.

"This is Chris," a deep male voice responded on the other end.

"Hi, this is Brett Axler. I am here for a 1:30 p.m. interview."

"Hey, Brett, I'll be right out."

Click.

A moment later, a tall, skinny gentleman walked through the door to greet me. Similar to the rest of the staff, he was wearing sports shorts, a t-shirt, and a backwards baseball cap.

"Hey, nice to meet you. I'm Chris." As he shook my hand, he looked at me and chuckled, "You didn't have to get all dressed up."

He led me up the stairs into a building with a pillar entrance surrounded by two enormous Eagle statues that towered over the steps and parking lot. "Yeah, that's about right for Philadelphia sports," I thought to myself as I thought about the intimidating reputation that Philadelphia sports fans maintained.

We headed down a long hallway plastered with pictures and memorabilia then entered a door labeled *ETN (Eagles Television Network).*

"We're currently building out our new studio," Chris explained. "With your background in AV for theatre I figured this would be a good place to start."

As we entered the studio, I saw lights and wires dangling from a hanging grid, set pieces spread about the floor, and a few guys set up with laptops and controllers on folding tables in the center of the room.

Chris introduced me to the team, "Hey, guys, this is Brett. He's a Drexel student with a background in AV."

To my surprise, all three guys stopped what they were doing and came over to introduce themselves. They asked me about my background in audio and video before quickly jumping to asking if I was an Eagles fan. Nervously, I told them I was a fan and that my whole family was lifelong Philadelphia sports fans, following up the comment admitting that I didn't know much about sports because I was more of a theatre geek.

One of the three guys jumped on the comment, "Ah, theatre geek! How well do you know lighting?!"

I smiled and said I knew a heck of a lot more about lighting than sports.

"Okay, good, take a look at this for me."

He walked me over to a console set-up on the folding tables in the middle of the room.

"We just got this console in and the three of us videots* are completely lost."

> Footnote: *Videot is a tech industry slang term for Video Idiot. While basic audio and lighting have played a key role in the technical production industry for decades, video has been an emerging technology over the past ten to fifteen years that changes rapidly and typically requires a different skill set than the average audio or lighting technician may hold. Video technicians often come from a different background than the audio and lighting technicians, such as TV, cinema, or film and may not have the same level of experience in audio or lighting, so they're typically made fun of and called videots.

I glared down at the console and smiled. Luckily it was one of the controllers I was very familiar with.

"SmartFade ML," I looked up at the guy. "What's going on with it?"

"Well, we preprogrammed it in the shop, and everything was working, but when we got here, we couldn't connect with the lights. Lights have power and nothing's changed. We verified all of the addresses match."

I peered at the console and pressed the down arrow to flip through the system's small menu to check a few settings. After sliding a few of the faders and checking that blackout wasn't enabled and it wasn't stuck in a weird cue, I got down on the floor and started following the wire path. The three guys and Chris stood there watching me as I troubleshooted the problem. I could feel them glaring at me, this college freshman all dressed up like I was ready for an interview with the CEO, crawling on his hands and knees sifting through power and data wires.

I had a feeling that this was a test. I could not understand any other reason why four guys who worked in broadcasting for an NFL team would be asking a college freshman to troubleshoot their brand-new studio lighting grid. After a few minutes I tracked down the DMX splitter box (the unit in a lighting system that distributes the data connection to all of the light fixtures) and noticed that its power was unplugged, meaning the data was not getting from the lighting console to the lights. I quickly plugged the box in and immediately saw all the lights flash, lighting up the studio. I headed back to the console and slowly dragged the master fader from 0 to 100 percent. The lights slowly faded up, and the studio came to life with color.

Chris chuckled, "Cool, are you available Monday for a press conference?"

To this day, I still have no idea if it was a test or not, but that's pretty much where the interview ended. I wasn't available the following Monday because of a work conflict at Fringe, but a week later, I found myself standing on the twenty-five-yard line of the Eagles end zone holding a backpack of batteries and water bottles supporting the wireless camera operators for team intros at the season home opener.

I didn't know it then, but I had just hit the first tipping point of my young career. Things were about to get pretty exciting.

 SHOW NOTES:

- Get personal business cards created and have them on you at all times. They don't need to be anything fancy. They just need to get the point across.
- Don't let the fear of rejection hold you back from making professional connections. Rejection can be scary to anyone, but what's the worst that can

happen? If you don't hear back or you get a no, it's not life-altering.

- It doesn't matter who you are talking to. Everyone, and I mean everyone, could be the connection to your next big break. Treat everyone you meet with equal respect.
- Stay in touch and keep your name relevant.
- Set up your LinkedIn profile and always keep it up-to-date. Even if you are not actively looking for a job, it will be there waiting for you when you need it. In the meantime, you never know who may come across your profile when you least expect it.
- Be patient. Some connections may take years to pay off while others pay off immediately. Even if it doesn't happen fast, at least you have the connection when you need it most.
- Set reminders to follow up. While remembering to follow up with someone about an opportunity a few months out may be seemingly simple, life gets in the way, things change, and it's easy to forget.

Chapter 7:

Physically Not Enough Hours in A Day (On Time Management and Learning to Say No)

"*There aren't enough hours in a day*" has to be one of the most overused lines, and it almost never accurately describes the situation it is being applied to. Earlier in the book, I touched briefly on how I managed my busy schedule in high school by charting every hour of the day, setting priorities, and having backup plans for when I got double-booked for an event. It was a flawless system that never failed me during my high school years, and I carried this same time management method into my freshman year of college. While my freshman year was fairly simple and didn't require much schedule management, sophomore year was a whole other ball game. Looking back at my calendar from the first week of sophomore year, here's a list of all of the commitments I had to manage in just one week:

- Six College Courses
- Strike and close out Fringe Festival
- Three days of work with the Eagles
- Two work halls in my college theatre
- Rehearsal for Temple University's production of *Spring Awakening*
- Pre-production call with 6abc for the Thanksgiving Day Parade
- DAK PAC first meeting of the year
- Yom Kippur in the middle of the week on a Wednesday ... why do you do this to us lunar calendar?!

Aside from the completely absurd context-switching required to manage work, school, and activities, this was the first week of my life I ever came close to physically running out of time. While I have no way to remember the exact number for sure, I guarantee I was drinking a minimum of five cups of coffee per day. While that took care of exhaustion from lack of sleep, all of the coffee in the world could not fix my inability to be in two places at the same time, physically running out of hours in the day even after pulling two all-nighters.

The hardest thing to admit about this situation is that it didn't stop me from scheduling many more upcoming weeks with a similar madness.

Unlike my senior year of high school when I burned out from stress and anxiety, no matter how crazy my schedule got that year, I stayed motivated by all of the new, exciting opportunities coming my way. While my body was physically incapable of pulling any more all-nighters, the combination of coffee and sheer motivation allowed me to keep powering forward. Fortunately for my career and bank account, my relentless schedule was paying dividends. Unfortunately, the case was not the same for my grades or school activities, which I found less exciting.

It wasn't long into the first semester of sophomore year before the cracks started to become visible. First it was in two of my classes: math and accounting. Midterms came and went—and so did my required 3.5

GPA. I received a warning from the university that I risked losing my scholarship if I was unable to get my GPA back up by the end of the year. For some reason, twenty-year-old Brett was not even the slightest bit concerned about this warning.

(I can tell you twenty-seven-year-old Brett who's still paying for this mistake on the fifteenth of every month wants to go back and slap twenty-year-old Brett across the face.)

But I digress.

After my GPA started to take a dive, the school activities that I didn't care much for started to do the same. That led to various warnings from the advisors overseeing the activities that I needed to better prioritize my time.

What in the world was wrong with me?!

While my education and social life were slowly deteriorating, my professional network and career was headed in the complete opposite direction. I was spending my weekends at Lincoln Financial Field working on the production team for Temple Football and Eagles games, the connections I made during the Fringe Festival were flourishing into work in the theatres all around the city, and the Office of Student Affairs had me in weekly meetings as the production advisor for all of the big events on campus.

I should have been torn between the strong positives and negatives that were happening in my life, but I didn't even remotely care about my C+ average and failing friendships because everything else was going so well. My logic at the time was that grades were not going to land me my first big job out of college; my connections and hands-on experience were. Ultimately, I was right. But to this day I am not proud of my grades, and I don't recommend anyone use that logic if you're on the verge of losing your scholarship due to poor grades. It will cost you more in the long run and make it very challenging to get accepted into graduate programs if that's the route you are planning to take.

As you may expect, I was only able to keep this up for so long before it all came crashing down. Luckily this time it wasn't a flaming explosion like the summer after my senior year. Ultimately, I ended up overbooking myself professionally and almost got fired from one of the shows I was hired to design audio for. Really, I think the only reason I didn't get fired was because I was able to find them an immediate replacement, and two years after that ordeal the same director called me back twice admitting that he couldn't find anyone else who mixed the show to his standards like I did. As flattered as I was, by that time I was smart enough to say no because I knew I didn't have the time or interest.

 Director's Note:
In the wise words of Steve Martin, "Be so good they can't ignore you." Not that I recommend overbooking yourself or using your reputation as a fallback for your poor time management skills, but typically you will be cut a lot more slack when you have a strong reputation of producing amazing work and being reliable.

 Director's Note:
Keep a short list of up-and-coming students and young professionals who show potential. When you're asked if you know anyone who may be a good fit for a position or role, it's much easier to reference a short list in the notes app on your phone than it is to pull the names out of thin air. This goes back to what I was saying about keeping in touch. There may be someone who is perfect for the position or role you are trying to fill but if you haven't seen or spoken to that person in a few years, the odds are that they won't immediately come to mind. Stay relevant and

keep your rolodex up to date! (I love the term rolodex ... my millennial is showing!)

Between almost getting fired from a show and being forced to turn down a paying job in order to make up my required hours in the university's theatre by mixing audio for the winter musical, I concluded that I needed to take a step back and reevaluate my focus.

Over winter break I talked to my parents about my career goals and got their input on the best path forward. In the span of less than eighteen months I basically had gone from two potential career paths to six—and I was trying to pursue every single one of them at the same time.

Priorities had to be set. Something had to go.

 Dɪʀᴇᴄᴛᴏʀ's Nᴏᴛᴇ:
Take time to evaluate your career priorities. Even if everything is going well and you don't feel overwhelmed, taking time to hone in on your career goals can highlight some areas that you can refocus or drop, allowing improvement of your work–life balance.

I decided the best way to go about prioritizing my schedule was to first hone in on what my current career goals were. At that point, I was still confident that my number-one goal was to eventually land at Disney designing the technology for their shows and nighttime spectaculars. This was just a year after I had met Gene working on the Thanksgiving Day Parade, and I had emailed back and forth with him a few times and seemed fairly confident that the educational and professional career path I was heading down would eventually lead me to accomplishing that goal.

Broadway was still a close second on my list of career goals, but coming off a year of working on twenty-two individual productions in less than ten months—and not enjoying many of them because they were not genres I liked—I was starting to have some concerns about putting too much more time and effort into my journey to Broadway. While working on the Fringe Festival, I noticed that being fully submerged in theatre full-time didn't give me room for an escape or mental break because theatre was my true passion. It was where I enjoyed escaping to when life got stressful, but if theatre was what was stressing me out, I didn't know where to head next.

I knew I definitely didn't want to go back to running a DJ business, so that was a no-brainer to mark as a low priority, and I had been actively trying to move away from it for most of the prior year anyway.

The last two potential career paths were both relatively new to me: concert production and sports broadcasting. I had worked on a small handful of professional concerts prior to college that I really enjoyed, from *Boys Like Girls* and *Good Charlotte* to this new pop-country star from Pennsylvania who was apparently close to breaking out. (I think her name was Taylor?) I enjoyed working on concerts but didn't know enough about them or the work involved to make a clear decision about whether it was something I wanted to pursue.

 Blocking Note:

Looking back I am so incredibly thankful I did not pursue a life producing concerts. I have worked on dozens of concerts over the years from small up-and-coming bands playing bars (That's how I first met Imagine Dragons!) to running venue technical operations when a big tour comes in and sells out 50,000 seats in a stadium two nights in a row. They all have been a blast to work on, but I commend anyone who can maintain any type of mental or physical normalcy living that life. It is not a career for the faint of heart.

As for sports broadcasting, I was having a blast working as an intern for the Eagles. It was a new and exciting experience in a world that I had never dabbled in before. After just six months, I felt like I had learned more than I had in the last three years of working on dozens of theatrical productions. There was definitely a lot of room to grow and new skills to learn that could potentially help me later in my career.

When I returned to school after winter break, I had a new plan. Everything DJ-related would be immediately deprioritized, I did not want to waste any time on a profession that I was already well-experienced in and had zero interest in ever returning to. The next gigs to be deprioritized were any theatre productions that did not pay and were not required as part of my program. Throughout most of high school and the first year and a half of college, I had spent a lot of time volunteering to work on theatrical productions in various positions. This was in part because I wanted to continue to grow my experience, but mostly because I loved (and still love) working on shows.

(Most shows. Les Mis *and* Spring Awakening, *if I never see you again, it will be too soon.)*

Along with cutting out all unnecessary theatrical work, I decided to change the concentration of my major from Entertainment Arts Management in Theatre to Entertainment and Arts Management in Television, Cinema, & Film. My thought behind this was fairly straightforward. I had been working in theatre for over ten years at that point. My craft and abilities as a technical director had taken me far beyond the average nineteen-year-old, and I wanted to start focusing my efforts elsewhere to grow skills outside of the theatre.

Blocking note:

I know that probably makes me sound pretty cocky. I'm not suggesting that I was some technical theatre prodigy at the age of nineteen. I definitely wasn't then, and I am not now, but I almost felt like an actor who was being typecast. My entire resume and portfolio revolved 100 percent around DJing and technical theatre, and I knew it was in my best interest to expand my skills beyond just those two industries. After 2020 when the entire entertainment industry was ravaged by the global pandemic, I can't be more thankful that I made the decision to grow my skill sets and experience in other industries. I highly recommend working in different industries during your career to diversify your skills as much as possible. Never stop learning and trying new things.

My prioritization plan along with my tightly managed schedule worked out fairly well for the rest of sophomore year. To this day I can't think of a time since then when I've had any issues turning down work opportunities in order to avoid overbooking my schedule. While I do enjoy spur-of-the-moment plans and just going with the flow in my personal life, when it comes to my career and professional obligations, I keep a military-like schedule. Every day starts and ends with me carefully combing through my schedule for the rest of the week to make sure I am well-prepared and am not double-booked.

 ## SHOW NOTES:

- There is plenty of time in a day. You have the same twenty-four hours as every other living being on this earth. Whether or not you have the time to complete all that you have set out to accomplish within those twenty-four hours completely depends on how you choose to prioritize your time.
- While throughout this book I harp on gaining as much hands-on experience as possible outside

of the classroom, and it is true that for many of us our GPA won't have any impact on our lives after graduation, it's still important to find an even balance between hands-on work experience and the classroom. Even if you're not relying on a minimum GPA for financial aid and you don't intend on applying to grad school, learning to set priorities and manage your time wisely will easily make you stand out in any career that you choose. Don't let them fool you. You will be amazed once you realize how unorganized the average adult is.

- Saying yes is important to gain access to new opportunities and skills that will help you grow personally and professionally but learning to say no is just as important. Choose how you spend your time wisely and don't overload yourself. As much as many of us wish we were able to harness our inner Hermione and be in two places at once, sadly, that just isn't the case. Set priorities for yourself. When a schedule conflict occurs, while it may not be the most ideal or fun decision, if you stick to your priorities, at least you know you've made the right decision for you.

- "Be so good they can't ignore you" ~ Steve Martin. While this is slightly out of context from the original intent of this quote, I find it to be a fair parallel. We're all human. We all make mistakes. Having a well-established history of being a hard worker with consistent results will typically lead to you being cut quite a bit more slack when you need it.

- Keep a short list of up-and-coming students and young professionals who show potential. When you're asked if you know anyone who may be a good fit for a position or role, it's much easier to reference a short list in the notes app on your phone than it is to pull the names out of thin air.
- Don't typecast yourself. Find other industries where your skills may be useful or look into developing skills in other industries that may interest you. The more diverse your skill sets and experience, the more jobs you'll qualify for.
- Take time to evaluate your career priorities. Even if everything is going well and you don't feel overwhelmed, taking time to hone in on your career goals can highlight some areas that you can refocus or drop, allowing improvement of your work–life balance.

Chapter 8:

You Want It? Go and Get It!
(On Thinking Outside the Box)

After Steve Job's death in 2010, his old interviews started to become popular on the internet, highlighting what a truly amazing innovator and futurist Jobs was. Among the famous interviews that surfaced was an old interview from 1994 in which Jobs spoke about his personal views on the secrets of life.

"When you grow up you tend to get told the world is the way it is and your life is to just live your life inside the world. Try not to bash into the walls too much. Try to have a nice family life, have fun, save a little money. That's a very limited life. Life can be much broader once you discover one simple fact: Everything around you that you call life was made up by people that were no smarter than you. And you can change it, you can influence it ... Once you learn that, you'll never be the same again." ~ Steve Jobs

Over the past few years of speaking to students and young professionals, I've come to the sad conclusion that along with the many other crucial life lessons that are rarely taught in school (like managing your personal finances and understanding the basics of taxes) how to market yourself to schools and employers is markedly absent. Some students were lucky enough to go to a high school or college that actually took a break from the ridiculous memorization of facts about the ships that sailed the ocean blue in the sixteenth century (all of which can be Googled and won't be relevant to most of us after we pass eleventh grade history) and instead took the time to teach us how to write a cover letter and resume. Even fewer students were lucky enough to attend a school that teaches interview preparation.

While I don't have many complaints about my education or school curriculums, I was not one of those lucky students who were taught any of the things I mentioned in the last paragraph in a formal classroom setting. However, I was fortunate enough to have some of the world's most amazing mentors teach me some of life's important professional networking and career lessons. I was taught how to file my taxes by my mom and neighbor, I was taught how to write and format a resume by one of my former technical directors, and, most importantly, I was taught how to market myself by my high school principal.

Throughout my education, I was always close with my teachers and school administrators. I was lucky to have some insanely talented and amazingly professional teachers and principals. In middle school, it was Mr. Morgan, my band director, my school's technology teacher, Mr. DJ, and superintendent, Dr. K. Between the three of them I had mentors to teach me more valuable life and career lessons as a middle schooler than most people learn by their college years.

In high school I had countless amazing teachers and administrators who mentored me and gave me opportunities to learn and grow my technology skills far beyond anything I could have learned in the classroom. To this day I genuinely believe that the teachers, staff, and administrators at Rancocas Valley Regional High School are the most influential people in my life I must thank (other than my parents) for me making it to where I am today.

And one of those key mentors was my principal, Mr. Booth. He and I were introduced my freshman year when he started overseeing the operation of the school's theatre and I was running the technology for the shows and events in the space. I didn't know it as a freshman, and maybe not even as a sophomore, but by junior year I came to realize that every question Mr. Booth asked me and every assignment he gave me was specifically crafted to challenge me and force me to grow.

Late in the fall term of my junior year, I was sitting in his office discussing college applications. This was just a few months after I had come back from Disneyland with my family, and I told him it was my number-one career goal to work for Disney designing their shows. I told him my parents had taken me to Drexel University for an open house and I was introduced to a program called Entertainment and Arts Management that seemed absolutely perfect for me. One of the adjunct professors had been a producer on the opening cast of *Beauty and the Beast* on Broadway and multiple alumni had landed jobs with Disney. I went on to explain that while I felt the program was a perfect fit for me, I did not have the grades or SAT scores to make the cut.

Mr. Booth peered over his glasses and stared at me with a blank look of confusion.

"According to who?" he asked.

"Well, according to the university's minimum GPA and SAT score requirements posted on their website," I replied.

He laughed, "Well they haven't met you yet."

I looked at him confused.

"Here's what you're going to do," he explained. "Over winter break you're going to gather all of the designs, photos, and details from the work you've done over the past few years—school shows you've designed lighting for, high-end clients you've provided production services to, and all the details about the company you own and operate. Take all that information and build a portfolio. I want it printed, professionally bound, and placed on my desk the day you return from winter break."

This is where his version of the story and mine differ slightly. According to him I rolled my eyes and complained that I didn't think a university was going to care about some high schooler's DJ company. Personally, I remember my reaction being something more along the lines of me giving off a visually apparent dread of spending winter break on a school assignment. Either way I listened to his advice and spent winter break building a fifteen-page portfolio that included everything from my CAD designs for shows to the template contracts I utilized for my production company clients. Before the end of break, I went over to the local supply store and I had them print a professionally bound version in full color.

When I returned to school in January, I headed right to Mr. Booth's office and placed the portfolio on his desk. He took about a minute to flip through the pages.

"Looks great, how many copies do you have?"

"The one you're holding," I sheepishly replied.

"Well, you're not trying to convince me! I already know what you're capable of," he said sarcastically. "You're applying to five schools, right?"

"Yes."

"Good, go get ten more copies made. Then go onto each school's website and find the mailing address for paper applications. Mail a copy to every school along with a personalized letter that includes your contact information and the reference number to your online application. Then go find the name and number of each program director. Call every one of them and ask to set up a meeting. Bring a copy with you to leave with each of them."

I did exactly as he described, and I was accepted to four of the five of the schools that I applied to with a scholarship offer from three of them. (I never finished the application for the fifth school.)

Blocking Note:

A few weeks before the end of my senior year of college, I had a meeting with Brian, the program director of my college major. Brian was the professor I interviewed with when I was applying to the program as a high school junior. As we reviewed my senior project and chatted about the journey from applicant to graduate, Brian walked over to the bookshelf in his office. He returned to his desk with the copy of my portfolio I had handed to him during my initial interview five years prior. Brian smiled and handed me the portfolio, "You made yourself stand out."

Dïrector's Note:

Creating a portfolio of your experience and work is an impactful solution to make yourself stand out whether you're a student applying to schools or a professional over twenty years into your career arguing for a promotion at work. A portfolio can be as simple as a five-to-ten-page paper or a slide deck of drawings, images, and screen-shots. Another option for the more technical folks is to create an online portfolio or website. Personally, I prefer the website because you can embed video content and link directly to resources or projects that you've worked on, plus it's easy to keep up-to-date and you can add the link directly to your LinkedIn, resume, and applications. No matter how you choose to build your portfolio, the goal is to make yourself stand out from the rest of the applicants and be memorable.

As Captain Barbosa so famously expressed in the first *Pirates of the Caribbean* film, "And thirdly, the code is more what you'd call **"guidelines"** than actual rules."

Every year I read staggering new facts about the number of qualified applicants who don't apply for a job because they don't believe they meet all of the qualifications listed in the job posting. While there are statistics that suggest this is more often the case with women applicants, I can say I've personally witnessed this in people of all ages, genders, races, and stages of their career. I am here to tell you to stop making this mistake!

What do you have to lose when applying to a job you think you may be underqualified for? Absolutely nothing!

What is the absolute worst thing that can happen? You don't hear back.

Is that really that bad? What is the second-worst thing that can happen? You hear back from the employer with a "thanks but no thanks."

What's the third-worst thing that can happen? They interview you and find that your skill sets don't meet their needs. This isn't exactly a bad thing though. Personally, I call that situation a win. Even if they don't say that they're going to keep your resume on file for a few months should a position pop up that you are better qualified for, you at least got some real-life interview experience, and that's worth its weight in gold. Plus, just landing the interview meant they saw some potential based on your application and resume. Congrats! Think about how many applicants don't even make it through the front door.

On the positive side, what's the best thing that can happen? You get called for an interview, they really like you, and they find that your unique skill sets or experience make up for any skills you lack. They decide that you're the best fit for the job and make you an offer. It's not that crazy of an idea. Trust me, these kinds of things happen every day!

Skills and experience are not everything. Just because the job posting says that the minimum requirements include the ability to navigate Salesforce or Adobe Cloud and you don't feel confident on either of those platforms (but you come with years of experience in 80 percent of the rest of the minimum required qualifications) does not necessarily mean that the employer will rule you out. They may end up finding that culturally you're the best fit for the team and decide to pay for your training on the platforms.

I'm not going to go deep down this rabbit hole here, but if I write another book about applications and interviews, there's going to be a solid chapter or two on cultural fit. *"Skills aren't everything"* is a term that you will likely hear quite a few times in your career. If you're working for an employer who believes this, they're probably a pretty good employer. On the other hand, if you're working for an employer who believes skills *are* everything, you may want to reevaluate your future in that company.

The short of it is, most skills are trainable (unless you're an Olympic athlete or a surgeon or in another profession that takes years of hard work, practice, and—in the Olympian's case—natural ability). From the use of a specific piece of software and computer programming to real estate sales and marketing, pretty much any skill is trainable. I'm not suggesting these skills are easy or quick to learn if you come with zero experience, but ultimately you can learn the same way everyone in those professions learned: studying, practice, and hard work.

Culture is a completely different beast. Nobody gets along with everybody. We've all had that classmate or coworker who drives us absolutely nuts. It may be because they're a slacker.

"You're a slacker McFly, you remind me of your father when he went here. He was a slacker too!" (Sorry, I warned you about the quotes!)

Or it may be for no particular reason; you simply just don't get along. Either way, every company and team has a culture, and simply put to avoid going down a crazy tangent, you can train someone on skills, but you can't train their personality to fit your team's culture.

This is all just to say that when you are applying and interviewing for a job, your skills and experience are not the only assets you are being graded on. Don't rule yourself out before you give the employer a chance to make that decision.

Aside from cultural fit, there's another crucial asset an applicant can offer that simply cannot be taught: passion. Everyone is passionate about something. Whether it's helping others, making discoveries in math and science research, or television and film, I guarantee there's something that gets your gears turning. There's a big difference between having an interest for something and being passionate about it. According to the dictionary, the definition of passion is a *"strong and barely controllable emotion."* As its definition suggests, passion is an emotional reaction.

***

During the 2020 NFL football season, teams and networks decided to pipe in crowd noise into the empty stadiums. There were a few reasons they did this, but one of the primary goals was to add energy to the broadcast. Imagine watching a football game and having it be as silent as a golf tournament.

Thrilling, right?

In order to make the crowd noise sound natural, the networks added a position to the game day audio crew that would control the level of crowd noise based on what was happening in the game. This required an operator to intently watch and judge every play of the game to decide how a normal crowd would react and quickly make the correct changes to the volume of the crowd noise.

While this may sound like a simple job and one that any football fan would dream of, it takes extreme concentration and does not leave any room for mistakes. It would be extremely obvious if a touchdown happened and the crowd remained at a murmur. On the contrary, if the crowd randomly went wild during a time-out, something may seem a little off to the viewers.

One of my coworkers was hired by the local network to run the crowd noise. He had been a contractor in the league for about ten years and everyone who worked with him knew he was one of the most passionate fans of the team that he worked for. While most of the operators hired to manage the crowd noise would simply ride the fader up and down between plays, my coworker was glued to the controls. His burning passion for the team and game was felt in the genuine reactions heard through the crowd noise. Rumor had it by the third week of the season he was the top operator in the league. It wasn't that he was talented, it wasn't that he was interested—he was passionate.

Let your passion show. It can be your greatest asset and ultimately what sets you apart from the rest.

Director's Note:
As someone who's been on a candidate review committee for many different positions over the years, I can personally attest to passion speaking louder than skills or experience. While of course being the most passionate candidate likely won't make up for you being far underqualified for a position, it absolutely can make you stand out above the rest of the candidates.

***

The Philadelphia Sports Complex is located on Broadstreet just outside of the Navy Yard in South Philly. The complex has a long, unique history from the early days of JFK Field and the Spectrum to Veterans

Stadium and the appropriately formerly named FU Center (stay classy, Philadelphia) and the twenty-first-century additions of Citizens Bank Park and Lincoln Financial Field. Over a dozen teams have called the historic sports complex home, along with tens of thousands of events and concerts. As of 2020, the complex still remains home to all four of Philadelphia's major league sports teams.

Early in my first year working for the Philadelphia Eagles, I came to realize that with all of the sports teams and stadiums centrally located, the sports complex community was incredibly small. Everyone from the two stadiums and the arena knew each other. From the front office and ops teams to dock operators, everyone was one giant family between the three venues *(a standard Philly kind of dysfunctional: like you to your face but not to your back and dare anyone who was not one of us talk crap about any of us and we'll all kick their butt).* The broadcast teams were similar, although our community stretched outside of the South Philly Sports complex to include the five Philadelphia universities, three major television networks, and the Union soccer team in Chester.

While hockey, basketball, baseball, and soccer all frequently overlapped one another with home games, football was almost always a solo event. This was mostly by design due to the complex's inability to physically handle the traffic, but also, it's the NFL, and as a ten-billion-dollar-a-year business, the league basically owns Sundays. Being the only game in town meant that no one missed it. The press cafeteria every Sunday home game was like a Philadelphia broadcasters' reunion. From the network hosts and directors to the producers for every professional and college team in town, everyone was there and, in Philly style, loud and proud.

As a college undergrad new to the sports broadcast community, I was in networking heaven. While I want to believe I was courteous and professional, at the end of the day, I was a nineteen-year-old who lacked tact. From the start I became friends with the camera ops and audio guys who I assisted as an intern. They were always very friendly and more than happy to introduce me to the producers from the other teams. Every time I had the chance to network with one of the directors or producers, I would quickly jump to asking if they were looking for any freelancers or interns. The responses were usually about a 60/40 split between being open to the idea and appreciating my young drive, while the rest didn't hide their frustration with my forward manner.

Director's Note:

Learning to read a room isn't easy for everyone. In fact, there are a ton of well-established professionals I've worked with who admit their poor ability to read a room. This is all part of being a good communicator, learning to listen and pay attention to a person's body language and tone while actively listening to the words they are saying. In my experience this just takes time and practice.

By the end of my second season, I had established a pretty good relationship with most of the producers and directors. While some were very direct and told me they simply did not have any openings on their production crews, others made it perfectly obvious with their mannerisms that they did not want to be bothered. Either way I appreciated the opportunity to meet them, and I hoped that time and dedication would lead to finding my way onto the teams.

It took about a year and half for the first opening.

While walking around the city with my roommates on a Saturday afternoon, I got a call from an area code I did not recognize. It was a producer from one of the local university's basketball teams.

"Hey, Brett, I remember you mentioning last year at the Linc that you were interested in picking up broadcast crew work around the city. Are you still interested?" she asked, sounding a little stressed.

"Absolutely, what positions are you looking for?" I replied.

"We're looking for an A1 to double as the DJ for the men's basketball season. Would you be able to manage both positions?"

Without taking a second to think, I enthusiastically replied yes.

"Okay cool, can you be here in an hour?" I could hear her gritting her teeth as she asked the question hopefully.

"Ha, yes, not a problem, on my way."

I hung up the phone and raced back to my apartment to change and grab my laptop.

The gig running audio and simultaneously DJing that basketball season turned out to be an incredibly interesting one that led to multiple leads in some crazy, unexpected ways.

The sports and entertainment venue industry is somewhat hard to describe to those who have never worked in it. A sports team's relationship to their venue varies from team to team and city to city. Some sports teams are the owner and operator of their venue, like Busch Stadium that's owned and operated by the St. Louis Cardinals. But a major league sports team owning and operating their venue is very rare. Most often the venue is owned by the city and operated by a third-party venue operator or the third-party venue operator both owns and operates the venue.

Philadelphia is home to one of the world's largest venue operation companies, Spectra Experiences. Formerly known as Global Spectrum, the company was a subsidiary of Comcast Spectacor, the venue management company founded by the late Philadelphia Flyers founder, Ed Snider. Snider led the early development of the Philadelphia Sports Complex back in the 1970s. After the original Spectrum arena, Snider's venue management company continued to grow across the city, country, and, eventually, the globe.

Agreeing to take on the gig as A1 and DJ for the university's men's basketball season inadvertently got my foot in the door with Global Spectrum because they were the venue managers of the arena that the team played in. Having just started my career in sports two years prior,

I did not yet understand the logistics of the sports venue management industry but, in my normal fashion, I got to know the staff at the venue and connected with many of them on LinkedIn.

A few months into the season was my twenty-first birthday. At that point it was the Eagles off season and Fringe was still a few months out, so my only source of income was $89 per game for DJing and running audio during the college basketball season. This was barely covering my rent, and the night of my birthday I had exactly $65 to my name. My roommates and I were getting ready to go out that night to celebrate when I got a phone call from Verizon. The caller ID on my cell phone literally said "Verizon". It was a courtesy call letting me know that my payment had bounced and if I paid right then and there, they would not charge me late fees. My bill was $59, I had exactly $65, and I was about to head out for my twenty-first birthday. Being the responsible nerd that I was (and still am), I paid the bill.

"$6 … I guess that will take care of the cover of at least one bar?" I thought to myself.

That night we headed out to a place called XFINITY Live! It was an indoor bar complex located in the center of all of the sports stadiums. Due to its convenient location it prided itself on being the official pre- and post-game party destination for all Philadelphia sports games. By the time we got there the Flyers game had just wrapped up and the place was packed. As I walked in, I noticed the impressive AV set-up for a sports bar. The ceiling was lined with moving lighting and there were concert-style speakers hanging from the ceiling surrounding an enormous LED screen that displayed live sports.

"This would be a neat place to work," I mumbled to myself as I mooned over the set-up.

At some point that night, I went up to the DJ booth and had a conversation with the DJ and technical director for the venue. The technical director was about to transfer to a different venue and they were actively looking for a replacement. They both handed me their business cards and when I woke up the next morning the cards were sitting with my wallet next to my bed. I reached over to grab the cards and noticed a familiar logo: Global Spectrum.

"You've got to be kidding me," I thought.

I texted both numbers, and about three days later, I was hired as the new technical director for the venue.

Blocking Note:

While XFINITY Live! was not owned or operated by Global Spectrum, they were an operating partner and therefore were part of the tight-knit venue management committee. Between my experience working for Global Spectrum, my experience working for the Eagles, and my references that included operating partners of their company, it was a quick interview process.

Ðirector's Note:

When applying for a job, curate your professional references to best match the job or company you are applying for. If you have the ability to use a current or past employee of that company as a reference, do it! While your favorite past boss or professor may be your go-to reference, think carefully about the job you are applying for. If you're well connected with a professional who works in the industry you are applying for, their word may be a bit more impactful than your former boss from when you were a cashier at the local convenience store.

About a year after accepting the position as the Technical Director at XFINITY Live! the sports industry in Philadelphia was keeping me fairly busy with freelance work. All of my networking was starting to pay off and I was working three to five games a week after school on top of managing the technical operations for the sports bar on the weekends. As it turned out, the bar scene in Philly was just as tight as the sports venues and after just a year of working for the largest sports bar in town, my name had gotten around to most of the big bars and they started hiring me to upgrade their AV systems and would call me in emergencies.

Blocking Note:

By my senior year of college, the bars calling me for emergency AV support started to get out of hand. I was getting three to five calls per weekend at all hours and bidding wars broke out between the bar managers bribing me to set their restaurant as a higher priority than the rest. The weekend of the World Cup, I got paid $450 for a fifteen-minute visit that turned out to be an unplugged cable. While this may sound completely absurd (trust me, it was), from the bar manager's point of view, if their restaurant was packed with paying customers expecting to watch the game and the TVs or game audio went out for even a few minutes, customers would likely rush out the door to the bar next door, equating to tens of thousands of dollars in lost sales. Once I took my new full-time job, I had to start referring the bar managers to my friends and classmates. Keep in mind, by this time I had been living in Philly for four years, so this type of demand was the culmination of four years of professional networking that was paying insane dividends.

I appreciated all of the work and opportunities, but the hours were starting to get to me, and I wasn't feeling like I was growing my career at all. With graduation only a year away, I started to get nervous that I was going to continue to be stuck in gig life after graduation, which would mean lack of benefits and job security. As much as I loved the free food and beverages and easy access to the city's top bars and clubs, I had much higher hopes for my career than being a mobile AV emergency room doctor crawling on sticky bar floors every weekend.

While moving down to Orlando to chase my career goals at Disney was still front of mind, I was loving my time in the sports industry and I really wanted to be the Technical Director of a professional sports venue.

I was fortunate to be living in Philadelphia with its central location in the Delaware Valley. There are over four dozen professional and college venues between Pennsylvania, New York, and Delaware. The odds of finding a full-time position at a venue without needing to relocate too far after college was a far more likely scenario than if I had lived in a more rural region of the country.

Every day I would browse TeamWorkOnline.com and WorkIn-Sports.com, the two largest sports venue job posting sites in the United States at the time. While I tried not to get discouraged, it was frustrating to realize that most venues were seeking someone with prior experience managing a sports venue. By this time, I had already spent years managing the technology for theatres, bars, and small performance venues, but I had never been the sole person managing the technology for a stadium or arena. I knew I was going to need a personal connection or inside referral to have a fighting chance of landing one of these positions. Along with continuing my job search, I constantly stayed in touch with my coworkers and connections at the local stadiums and arenas, letting them know I was on the hunt.

One morning I got a notification for a job that had just been posted. It was the Opening Audio Visual and Information Technology Manager at an arena that was under construction about forty-five minutes outside of Philadelphia. I immediately jumped on my computer to research the venue and see who the owners and operators were. As I was scrolling through the first page of Google results, I had two email notifications pop up in the corner of my screen, one from my school's program director and the other from one of the technical directors of the sports complex. They had both forwarded me the posting. My heart started to race as I read the job description.

They were seeking a candidate with three to five years of experience managing technology for sports, events, and other live entertainment. Requirements included experience in AV management, LED display operation and maintenance, team leadership, crew scheduling, and experience on a lengthy list of specific technology brands. As I looked over the requirements and preferred qualifications, I couldn't help but think I was the perfect candidate for the job.

Director's Note:

Be true to yourself. It's not being arrogant if it's true. You don't have to go around bragging but there's nothing wrong with being confident if it motivates you to chase your dreams.

It was a minor league sports arena with major league facilities. They were seeking a candidate who was well-rounded in both technology and people management. The arena was not an ideal location for most people. And, bingo, it was operated by Global Spectrum.

I skipped every class that day to send dozens of emails, call every connection I had in Global Spectrum, and, of course, apply for the job. Unfortunately, because the arena was still under construction, most of the operating staff had not yet been hired. This meant that most of the people I might have had a chance of being remotely connected to on LinkedIn were not yet hired. I did not have any first- or second-degree connections with anyone on LinkedIn so I had to try extra hard to find out who the hiring manager was. My number one goal was to find their name and email address so I could contact them directly.

 DÍRECTOR'S NOTE:
I will always recommend being the squeaky wheel while also setting limits to not come across as obnoxious or pushy. Finding out who you know in a company and trying to connect with the hiring manager will usually help you at least get your resume to the top of the pile if not give you a fighting chance of landing an interview. When you apply online, especially on the common websites, you are normally one of a few hundred applicants. You could have the most impressive resume in that pile, but between the sheer number of applicants and the algorithms that reject resumes before they even make it to anyone's inbox, the odds are always stacked against you. You absolutely have to make your name known and have human resources or the hiring manager specifically look for your resume in the pile.

Every company and industry is different but the difference between too loud and not loud enough is always a very thin gray area. In the sports broadcast industry, I've almost always been successful reaching out to employers directly and expressing interest. Of the eleven teams and venues I have had the pleasure of working with or receiving offers from, there were only two that outright rejected me for my persistence in reaching out. (I no longer fault myself for those two failures after I found out that the producers who rejected me at both those venues have since been let go for unfair hiring practices.)

After a few dozen phone calls, I found out that the hiring manager for the position was a former employee of the general manager of the college venue where I mixed audio for the men's basketball season. Bingo.

About two months later, after a dead car battery almost made me miss the interview and my friend forced me out of my pity party and demanded that I borrow her car, I started the job as the Audio Visual and Information Technology Manager on the opening team of a $280-million-dollar professional sports arena. I was twenty-one years old.

 ## SHOW NOTES:

- Don't self-reject. Just because you don't meet 100 percent of the requirements for a posted job doesn't mean you don't stand a chance of being hired. The employer may find that your other skills or passion for the work make up for the skills or experience you lack. Don't reject yourself before you allow the employer to make that call.

- Make yourself stand out. You may be one of a thousand candidates and one of thirty interviews. Find ways to separate yourself from the rest and make yourself memorable.

- A great way to make yourself stand out is by creating a portfolio. It doesn't have to be anything fancy. A simple packet, deck, or website that shows off your experience is already more than what the average applicant will provide.

- Learn to read the room. Social cues are hard for everyone and much harder for some of us than others. Learning to be an active listener will teach you that there's a lot more to hearing than what's coming out of the person's mouth. Learn to listen to tone of voice and body language as well.

- When applying for a job, curate your professional references to best match the job or company you are applying for. If you have the ability to use a current or past employee of that company as a reference, do it!
- Building your professional network takes time. Be patient and stay persistent.
- Be true to yourself. It's not being arrogant if it's true. You don't have to go around bragging but there's nothing wrong with being confident if it motivates you to chase your dreams.
- Get your resume to the top of the pile. Reach out to any connections you have with the company you are applying to and ask for an introduction. If you don't have any direct connections to the company, go on LinkedIn and look for second-degree connections. The worst thing that can happen is you don't receive a response.

Chapter 9:
You're Never Going to Fly If You Don't Take the Leap (On Risky Decisions)

W e are all faced with tough career decisions at some point. What those decisions are and when they take place make some of them a lot harder than others.

Typically, when you're young, you have fewer responsibilities tying you down. You may just have yourself to take care of, and odds are you have a lot less to lose. Once you're older and more established in your personal life and career, even the little decisions suddenly become big ones. Keeping this in mind, while some decisions may seem scary and feel like you're taking a leap of faith, consider how much harder that same decision might be if you wait five for ten years.

Taking it a step further, how would you feel if you turned down the opportunity because it didn't feel like the right time or you were simply scared to take the risk and the opportunity never presented itself again?

Everyone's situation is different, and you should always carefully assess the risks, but in my experience, the term has always remained true: You're never going to fly if you don't take the leap.

***

A few weeks after I accepted the new position with the arena was the annual Thanksgiving Day Parade. Similar to the previous three years, I was asked by the parade staff to coordinate a group of students to work as production assistants on the effects and props crew for the parade.

During rehearsal, I had a chance to catch up with Gene, the Disney producer who I'd worked with the past few years. As we stood outside the production trailer waiting for rehearsal to start Gene looked over at me and asked, "You're graduating this year, right?"

"Yeah, I should be done by June," I replied, knowing what his question was implying.

"So, you gonna make the move?" It was the same question he asked me every year, implying that I should make the move to Orlando to chase my dream of working for Disney.

"Well, I actually just accepted a new position running the technology for a new arena up in Allentown," I cautiously replied.

"Okay, you've got my number," he grabbed his clipboard and headset and headed toward the parade route.

Even though I fully expected his question, it really made me question myself and my decision to go so off course from my biggest career goal. I had already turned down the Disney College Program a couple years prior to continue pursuing opportunities in sports broadcasting. I hadn't worked the Fringe Festival this past year due to being too busy at the sports complex. I had gone from working ten to twenty theatrical shows per year to just two.

Was I just chasing money?

Was I really happy doing what I was doing?

Was I actually having a positive impact on the world or people's lives?

Was I going to regret never chasing my dreams of working for Disney or Broadway?

Each question made me feel like I was one concern closer to an all-out existential crisis.

 Blocking Note:

I know I was not alone in having these types of concerns at the age of twenty-one. In fact, I still have those same concerns from time to time. It's completely normal to experience self-doubt and question whether you are making the right decisions for your future when you are in high school, college, or even a few years into your professional career. In retrospect I can confidently say that it really didn't matter which path I chose to concentrate on at that point in time, as long as I continued to learn and grow while keeping all of my professional connections intact. Opportunities will come and go, but knowledge and experience are yours to keep forever.

Work at the arena was intense. I had worked in plenty of arenas and on dozens of sporting events and concerts but never in a brand-new venue. From day one we were hosting hockey games back-to-back with concerts and filling the arena to capacity multiple nights per week. On top of managing all of these events, we were training new crew members, working out the kinks in the AV systems, and meeting with contractors around the clock to work our way through the 800+ item punch list. It was kind of like living on, working in, and hosting 10,000 guests on a moving cruise ship all while it was still being built. Don't get me wrong, I loved it. I was thriving on the sheer ambiguity of arriving to work every day having absolutely no idea what would be thrown at me.

Aside from opening the arena, I was still finishing up school and living in Philadelphia, sixty-five miles away from the venue. Luckily my professors and academic advisor had worked with me to schedule all online hybrid classes so I did not physically have to be on campus for most classes. But this did not help my commute from my apartment or the length of my average day.

Allentown, Pennsylvania is just under an hour outside of Philadelphia without traffic. There's only one viable way to get to and from Allentown from Philadelphia—the Schuylkill expressway to the Northeast Extension. More commonly known to Philly folks as the "Sure kill expressway," the Schuylkill is a high-speed two- to eight-lane highway on the Northwest outskirts of Philadelphia. On the average weekday, traffic starts backing up by 5:15 a.m. and by 6 a.m., it's bumper-to-bumper traffic well through lunch before it resumes for the afternoon rush hour and doesn't clear until late into the evening.

My commute without traffic was about forty-five minutes. My commute with traffic could be anywhere from two to four hours. If I left my apartment in Philly on a weekday a minute past 5:15 a.m., I would not make it to work for the 9 a.m. team meeting. In the afternoons, if I left the arena any time before 7 p.m., I would be sitting in two to three hours of bumper-to-bumper traffic. In order to manage this, my average day looked something like this:

- *4:15 a.m.: Wake up, shower*
- *5:00 a.m.: Walk six blocks to my car and pray it started in zero-degree weather*
- *6:30 a.m.–9:00 a.m.: Arrive at work, work on schoolwork*
- *9:00 a.m.–12:00 p.m.: Project closeout meetings with contractors*
- *12:00 p.m.–1:00 p.m.: Lunch, gym*

- *1:00 p.m.–3:00 p.m.: Production meetings, AV maintenance*
- *3:00 p.m.–5:30 p.m.: Pre-game broadcast prep with crew*
- *5:30 p.m.–6:00 p.m.: Crew meal, doors open for fans*
- *6:00 p.m.–9:00 p.m.: Hockey game, concert, 10,000 screaming fans*
- *9:00 p.m.–10:00 p.m.: Post-game show, wrap*
- *10:00 p.m.–11:00 p.m.: Commute home*
- *11:00 p.m.–12:00 a.m.: Finish homework*
- *Repeat*

While this schedule was absolutely absurd, there were quite a few weeks when it was even worse.

Similar to airplanes, arenas and stadiums are typically only making money when they have guests in them. When there aren't any guests in the building, they're basically just very tall warehouses with abnormally high utility bills. In order to combat this, arena owners try to keep the building occupied with events as many days of the year as possible. However, events take time to load in and out. Every venue varies slightly depending on the size and experience of the transition crew, but typically when an arena flips from a hockey to a basketball game, it can be done in anywhere from five to eight hours. The transition from either sport to a concert has even more variability depending on the size and experience of the concert's touring crew and the local stagehands.

No matter how long it takes to flip the arena from one event to the next, it's typically calculated in hours instead of days. In a major league arena like the Wells Fargo Center in Philadelphia (home to both a hockey and a basketball team) it's common for the arena to be flipped mid-day between an afternoon game for one sport and an evening game for the other followed by an overnight transition for a concert the next day only to host hockey again the day after. *(Remember when I said working in concerts wasn't for the faint of heart?)*

Most venues that are this busy have multiple transition crews and management teams. This isn't to say they don't have to work the occasional twenty-hour shift but it's uncommon to work more than twenty-one days in a row without a break. This is not the case when working in a new venue. *(Trust me, I've done it a few times now.)*

Between January and April the first year the arena was open, my team and I worked seven days a week averaging a seventy-eight-hour workweek not including commute time. *(Yes, I was a salary employee.)* There were eleven occurrences when events were scheduled so tightly back-to-back that there wasn't enough time for me to drive home, shower, and get back in time, so I slept on the floor of my office and showered in the green room.

While the schedule was absolute madness, even with all of the stress and frustration, I appreciated having the opportunity to be part of the production and learn so many valuable lessons. Aside from the lessons in venue and time management, the main lesson I took away from that never-ending opening was confidently knowing that I did not want to work those kinds of hours for the rest of my life. It was a thrilling job, with plenty of rewarding attributes that many people would love to have, but even at twenty-two, I knew that I valued my health, sanity, and free time more than the thrilling experiences that came from a job like that.

Over the years I have crossed paths with dozens of professionals in the sports and venue operations management industry who find their jobs fulfilling and manage to live their lives around work. They love what they do, and most of them cannot imagine doing anything else. I commend all of these folks for their service and dedication to the sports and entertainment industry. For me, this was the beginning of the end of my time in sports venue management—or so I thought. (More on that later.)

Over the following months, I started to lose interest in the daily work in the venue. My team was absolutely amazing. They made the job worth showing up for, but I knew deep down that this was not the career path I wanted to continue down.

It was a weird feeling having spent the better part of four years working my way into and up the ranks of the professional sports industry, always focusing on landing my first job as a technical director of a venue, only to get there and discover it was not actually what I wanted at all. I was bummed that the job was not what I thought it was going to be, but I was also glad I gave it a try and learned a ton of new skills while working alongside some of Philly's finest professional sports venue leaders.

 Director's Note:
Learning what you don't want to do is just as important as learning what you do want to do. High school and college are the times to try everything (almost everything). Society's practice of pressuring sixteen-year-old juniors to decide what they want to do with the rest of their life is a tall order for young adults who have never spent a day in their perceived career of choice. Then to follow that choice with four or more years of school and potentially tens of thousands of dollars in student loan debt is just setting them up for failure. Take advantage of your status as a student to try everything. So, you think you want to be a cardiologist? Have you ever spent a day shadowing a cardiologist? Reach out to the local university hospital and do just that. You may find out that you don't like the sight of blood or being on your feet talking to patients for twelve-hour shifts. You just saved yourself six to eight years of school. Now move on to your next career choice and do the same. Reach out and shadow a professional in that position.

Blocking Note:

While I don't go into it in much detail in this book, shadowing a professional at work was actually what led me to deciding against working backstage on Broadway, along with a few other career goals I had in grade school. Growing up outside of New York City, I had the opportunity on multiple occasions to take backstage tours with the crew members. On those tours I asked a lot of questions and got insight into what their daily jobs looked like and I realized that pushing "Go" on a lighting console or operating a follow-spot eight shows per week was not how I wanted to be involved in the theatre. This revelation led me to pursue lighting design and audio engineering as other alternative career paths. While I would still love to work on Broadway one day, at least I already have a few positions ruled out.

By the time the winter rolled around I was having full-blown seasonal depression. My morning commute would start in the dark with temperatures below zero, I would arrive at the arena to work in a dark, windowless control room with indoor temperatures in the fifties, and by the time I got home it was already dark again. The hours in the car alone followed by hours alone in the control room on days there weren't events in the building exacerbated the problem. To this day I have notes on my phone that I wrote to myself during that time to remind myself that I never want to feel that alone again.

Of the dozens of shows, concerts, and events that we hosted that first year at the arena, there was one show that I was most excited about. Surprise, surprise, it was FELD's Disney On Ice. While most of my coworkers did not share this excitement and used the week as a break from the normal stresses of hockey and back-to-back concerts, I was ecstatic to be a part of the production. Although the show was not produced by Disney, just being surrounded by performers, technicians, and like-minded people for the week brought excitement and passion to my job again for a few days.

While loading in the show, I had the opportunity to meet the crew and pick their brains about their jobs and life on the road. There were stagehands who were fresh out of college working their first tour, department leads who had spent the last five to ten years on the road, and production office folks who had been on the road for over a decade and toured with their significant others. Everyone I talked to, no matter what their position was or how long they had been on the road, had one thing in common: They loved touring and could not see themselves doing anything else. They were one big family all working toward the same goal: putting on the show.

The final night of load-in before the first performance I was sitting at the front-of-house console talking with the show's lighting lead, Greg. He was a young professional who had only been on the road a few years. I was asking him about his background and how he got to heading up the lighting department on a well-known national tour. Greg shared a bit about his background in theatre and his passion for lighting before sharing that he had always had a love for Disney. He mentioned that he would like to work in the parks one day but was taking advantage of being young and single to travel the country on tour. I shared that making it down to Disney to work on their shows was a dream of mine as well and that I had a few connections who worked in the parks in Orlando. When he asked why I hadn't made the move yet, I realized I could not come up with a good answer.

That week we hosted seven performances of the show. As I watched each performance, I listened to the crowd's explosive applause as each of the Disney characters skated on to the stage. Hearing the roaring crowds brought me right back to my days working full-time in theatre.

While I may have just been a small supporting role of the production, just knowing that I played any role in putting the smiles on the faces of tens of thousands of audience members made the long, crazy hours well worth it. By the last day of shows, I was updating my resume, and on the drive home I started to rehearse for the phone call I knew I had to make.

Director's Note:

Greg had the right idea. He was young and single, so he took advantage of the unique time in his life to explore the world. Whether you would like to go on tour, work on a cruise ship, or travel the world as a YouTuber, there's no better time to do it than when you're young. You'll likely be working long, awful hours and not make great pay to start but you will get to travel, meet people of different cultures, and gain life experiences that you will take with you for the rest of your life.

Blocking Note:

Just a few years after our initial conversation, Greg reached out to let me know he had applied to Disney. I submitted a referral for him, and we ended up being coworkers for the better part of three years.

The following day I arrived back at work to find an empty arena. Other than hockey practices, the venue was dark for two days and we weren't scheduled to have fans until mid-week. I sat at my desk thinking about the conversation with Greg. He and his team were off to the next city to put on another half-dozen shows for an audience-packed arena while I sat in a dark control room backing up media files. His unit was scheduled to perform in thirty-seven cities over the following months where they would have the chance to meet countless people, explore new places, and perform for hundreds of thousands of guests. In that same period of time, I would be commuting back and forth from the same building over 250 times and working with the same eleven people.

During lunch I walked down the block to the local park. It felt freeing to get out of the dark control room and see some sunlight. I took a seat on a bench and stared down at my phone nervously. It was so cold that my breath was fogging up my phone as I thumbed through the numbers.

After just half a ring I heard a voice pick up on the other end, "This is Gene."

"Hey Gene, it's Brett Axler. How's it going?" I murmured with hesitation

"Hey, it's good. How's the weather in Philly," Gene laughed, knowing all too well that it was below freezing.

"Ha, yeah, it's like nine degrees," I replied, "yeah, so uh, I was thinking, it's time to make the move."

"Well, it's about time!" Gene responded excitedly. "Send me your resume."

 ## SHOW NOTES:

- You're never going to fly if you don't take the leap. While the career decision you are contemplating may seem scary, if it is going to provide you opportunities that you cannot possibly get from your current position, it may be the risk you have to take in order to achieve your goals.
- Typically, the longer you wait in life to make big career decisions, the more life tends to get in the way. Don't assume there will be a more convenient time in the future. The opportunity may never present itself again.

- Learning what you don't want to do is an incredibly important part of your career journey. Use every experience—the good, the bad, and the ugly—as a way to learn what you value most in your career and work–life balance. If you can't see yourself doing what you're doing for the rest of your career, there's no better time than now to develop a plan to get yourself the education or experience necessary to take the next step.

Chapter 10:

Stepping Down in Rank to Move Up in Company

I t is very rare to come across someone who has achieved great success in their career by following a straight line. Gone are the days when people graduate from college, land their first job, and stay with that employer for their entire career. These days, it's not just common but expected that young professionals will change employers a few times in the years after graduation.

While changing employers has benefits like building diversity and experience in your resume, not all employers are created equal, and transitioning from one employer to another may mean taking a step down in rank. If you've worked your way up the ranks in a small company, it doesn't necessarily mean that a larger, more well-known organization will be ready to hire you at the same level. When you join a larger organization, it often means a step down in rank.

Now, you may be thinking, "But I've got all these years of experience! Why should I have to take a step down and repeat the work

I've already accomplished? I have so much experience to bring to the team!"

While that may be true, the Fortune 500 company you are joining has likely been around since before you were born and you have to put time in to prove yourself and earn their respect. Trust me, you're not alone in thinking that way. After letting the door hit me on my way out a few times in my early career because of my young ego, I can confidently say that you always have more to learn. No one is too good to put their time in. No matter how much experience you bring to a team, you are being welcomed into someone else's home, and you will have to put in the time to earn the respect of your team.

This tends to be a little more obvious when folks are joining a team on the frontlines, but this is even more crucial when being hired to lead a team that was established before you got there. Just because you are the leader of the team does not mean you get a hall pass on putting your time in. You have to earn the respect of your team just like anyone else. I have had leaders who gained the respect of the team within days, and I've had leaders who never earned the respect of their team and were pushed out in their first ninety days.

Remember, people don't leave jobs; they leave managers.

When you face a decision like changing companies, it may seem like an enormous deal and you may question whether it's the right decision. That is completely normal, and you should be asking yourself that question before making any quick decisions. Changing companies and relocating for work can be hard enough. Add a change in rank into the mix that may affect your personal finances and now you've gone from having a lot to think about to feeling like the weight of the world is on your shoulders. I've been there a few times. Let's talk about how to handle it.

First, take a deep breath and try to see the forest through the trees. You've got your entire career ahead of you. Aside from doing something completely irrational that destroys your reputation across an entire industry, you can almost always go back to your roots if the move doesn't work out. This leads me to what just may be the most important lesson in this entire book:

 Director's Note:
Never burn any bridges, and I mean NEVER. This is a term you have hopefully heard your entire life. Never burning bridges should be a rule you follow in everything you do both in and out of your professional life. Whether it's leaving an employer in good standing so you can return one day or treating your waitress with respect, I implore you to treat every person you meet in life with equal respect. You never know when they might be the person saving your butt.

Even if you never intend to return to the company you are leaving, you never know when you may run into your coworkers again. And that doesn't just include your boss or teammates. You may walk into an interview one day to see your former intern sitting across the table. Trust me, crazier things have happened.

Next, you should ask yourself what your end goal is.

- Where do you see yourself in five years?
- Are the position and company going to provide you with skills and experience to help achieve that goal?
- Will this company look more valuable on your resume than your current one?

These questions aren't always going to be easy to answer but taking the time to think about them will help you focus on whether taking the position makes sense. It's easy to be dazzled by a company, job title, or location, but if a position won't add skills or experience that help you achieve your career goals, you have to decide whether it's worth the risk or not.

***

My freshman year of college, I decided to apply for the Disney College Program. I figured it would be a good way to get my foot in the door and gain experience that could help me land a job with the company. I had always heard wonderful things about the program and many entertainment employers would specifically look for applicants who had Disney experience.

During the application process I had to choose three different lines of business I would like to work in. The options ranged from custodial and food and beverage to parking and guest services among other frontline operations positions. Entertainment was listed as an option but it was specifically for performers and it required an audition. Having already had years of experience working in technical theatre and aiming to land a position working on the shows at Disney, I was specifically looking for a position that would allow me to gain experience in their technical department. After speaking to a recruiter, I was notified that technical operations were not an option for college program students, but she assured me that it would be a great experience either way and that I could choose to leave my position preferences blank.

I ended up doing exactly that and figured I would let the recruiting team review my application and put me wherever they felt I would be the best fit. After two phone interviews and a few weeks of waiting, I got a call from the recruiter congratulating me on being offered a position in parking operations as a tram driver. The position was a six-month contract at the Disneyland Resort in Anaheim, California. It paid less than $8 per hour, they didn't provide housing, and I would have to pay for all of my travel and lodging expenses.

To say this was a gut punch was an understatement. There I was, a freshman in college with a dream of working for Disney and an offer right in front of me, but it could not have been more wrong for me. If I took the position, I would have had to take two terms off of school, delaying my graduation by at least six months. Moving across the country would have cost me more than I would have made during the entire duration of my contract. And the cost of living in Anaheim for six months would have cost me about three times as much as I was being offered.

It was a tough decision, but after many conversations with my college professors and parents, they assured me that Disney was a very large company and turning down an offer from the college program would not hurt my chances of finding a more appropriate position with the organization in the future.

In retrospect, this was an easy decision for me. While everyone's situation is different and the Disney College Program is an absolutely fantastic career decision for most college students, it just did not make sense for me.

So, let's walk through the rationale for my situation.

Where did I see myself in five years?

My five-year goal at the time was to land a job with the Walt Disney Company. Taking a position with the company would have allowed me to get my foot in the door—but at what expense? I would have had to delay my education, take out more loans, and pause all of my work that was already providing me with valuable experience.

Was that position and company going to provide me with the skills and experience to achieve my goal?

Not exactly. While I would have gained valuable experience learning the culture of The Walt Disney Company and how to provide world-class customer service, working in parking operations did not directly correlate to my career goals. Staying where I was, working in theatres and stadiums around Philadelphia, would provide me with more valuable skills and experience that would help me land the job I was aiming for with the company later.

Would that company look more valuable on my resume than my current one?

Arguably, no. Even though you might think that having the The Walt Disney Company on my resume would be valuable when a recruiter from The Walt Disney Company reviewed my application in the future, having diverse experience from other companies such as Comcast and the NFL ultimately played a key role when I was offered a full-time position a few years later. Those experiences from other companies continued to pay dividends during my time at Disney when I had experience I could not have gained anywhere within the company.

Again, everyone's situation is different, and you have to make the decision for yourself. Personally, I highly recommend the Disney College Program and professional internships. Had I known about the Disney Parks Live Entertainment Technical Internship at the time, I would absolutely have applied and accepted had I been offered a position, no matter what the pay was.

***

Fast-forward four years. As Gene requested, I sent him my resume and began the nerve-racking wait to see if I would get called for an interview. Gene reminded me that I was going to have to be patient as the hiring process could be a little slow. During the weeks of waiting, all of the memories from applying and interviewing with the college program years earlier began to increase my anxiety. I was concerned that the recruiter was going to see that I turned down a position before. I was nervous that they were not going to be interested in me because I had changed the concentration of my major from theatre to television and film. I was absolutely terrified that they were going to offer me a position that did not make any sense for me again and I would have to decide whether to turn down an offer for the second time. It was an anxiety-filled few weeks and to make matters worse I couldn't talk to anyone about it because I didn't want my current employer to find out that I was considering leaving and I didn't want my friends and room-mates to know that there was a chance that I was moving out of town until I at least knew I had an offer.

Leading up to the first interview, I reached out to a few of my friends who had interviewed with the company before. I asked what I should expect to be asked and if they had any tips for me. There was one tip that I kept hearing over and over: *Practice smiling with your voice.* Disney is known for their world-class customer service. Being friendly and smiling may as well be a job requirement. Whether you're being greeted by a security cast member at the front of the Magic Kingdom or talking on the phone with a vacation planner at the reservation center, you can expect to be greeted with a smile. While I wouldn't count on your smile alone landing you a job with Disney, it sure doesn't hurt to prove to the recruiter that you know how to smile with your voice when talking to them on the phone.

After a few interviews and what felt like an eternity of anxiety, I was offered a position in the Technical Entertainment Department at Disney's Animal Kingdom. While it didn't pay well and the position required me to step down from being manager back to working as a frontline employee, the position checked all of the boxes for my five-year goal. It got my foot in the door for the technical entertainment department, I would gain skills and experience that would help me achieve my career goals, and the company would look more valuable on my resume than my current one.

I began to research the cost of living in Orlando and found that while I would be cutting it close financially, it wasn't impossible. I would be taking about a 55 percent pay cut, but my student loans were still in deferment. I would be saving about 30 percent on cost of living, and there wasn't any state income tax in Florida. I ran the offer by my parents and a few of my mentors and received overwhelming feedback that I should absolutely take the offer.

There was about a four-month gap between the time I was offered the job and my start date. During that time, I decided to make a few moves that paid off really well for me in the long run. I cut back on expenses in order to save as much money for the move as possible. Between packing lunch instead of buying and avoiding multiple trips per day to Tim Hortons and Dunkin, I was able to increase my savings. In anticipation of the money I knew I was going to be spending on travel living 1,000 miles away from my family, I decided to apply for an airline credit card to start earning miles. Lastly, I reached out to all my old connections around the bars in Philly and told them I was available for AV tech support for the following months.

By the time summer rolled around, I had put in my notice at work, announced to my friends and family that I would be leaving, and my mom and I jumped in the car for the drive down to Florida.

 SHOW NOTES:

- Careers are not a straight line. You will likely have to change roles, companies, and rank multiple times before you gain the experience necessary to land your dream job.
- Not all employers are created equal. A frontline job in a nationally known company may look more

impressive on your resume than a management job in a small firm. Stepping down in rank may be what you have to do in order to get your foot in the door in a larger organization.

- Everyone has to put their time in. Whether you're joining a team as a frontline employee or the leader, you are being welcomed into someone else's home. Take your time and make a strong effort to earn the respect of your team.

- NEVER BURN ANY BRIDGES. You never know when someone might be the person saving your butt in the future.

- Avoid being blinded by the glitz and glamour of a position, title, or company. Ask yourself how the move fits into your five-year plan, whether it will provide the skills and experiences you need, and if it looks better on your resume than your current position.

- You have your entire career ahead of you. As long as you keep your connections intact and keep your skills up-to-date, you can always head back to your roots if the risk doesn't work out.

Chapter 11:

Dreams Take Hard Work to Come True

"So many of our dreams at first seem impossible, then they seem improbable, and then, when we summon the will, they soon become inevitable." ~ Christopher Reeve

We all have dreams. We all have aspirations. Some of us were lucky enough to grow up hearing that we could achieve any dream we set our mind to. Some of us were lucky enough to have mentors to guide the early stages of our journey. And few of us were told the truth about what we would have to sacrifice and how hard we would have to work to achieve our dreams. Then there are those of us crazy enough to believe we can actually make our dreams a reality.

It's easy to dream. That's the reason we all have dreams. But turning dreams into reality is no easy feat. Some dreams may be completely within your control and just take time and effort but other dreams may only be partially in your control. You might work as hard as you can to achieve them but the stars don't align. Then there are dreams that are seemingly impossible because they are completely out of your control. Personally, I find those dreams to be the most fun to chase because you can go in with low expectations and easily enjoy the journey. These are typically also the victories that stand out as your biggest achievements.

No matter what your dream is and whether or not it is within your control, it will be your perseverance, dedication, and passion that lead to making that dream a reality.

I grew up with many dreams. When I was young, I dreamed of being a famous actor or soundtrack composer. As I moved into technical theatre, I dreamed of being a lighting designer on Broadway. As I was introduced to Disney's groundbreaking technology, I dreamed of being an Imagineer. Now I dream of having the financial means to be a philanthropist for arts and science education and being a Broadway producer.

No matter how my dreams have grown and changed over the years, I have always remained dedicated to having a plan for how to make those dreams a reality. When I wanted to become a soundtrack composer, I started by reaching out to my music teacher and asking him for advice. I spent years learning as many instruments as I could and researching how famous composers like John Williams and Hans Zimmer got to where they are.

As my dreams turned to technical theatre and lighting design in high school, I started to chart out my journey to Broadway by meeting as many current professionals as I could get in touch with. Whenever I attended a show, I would walk right up to the audio or lighting technicians during intermission and ask about their jobs and how they got there. I carried business cards with me. (Yes, as a high schooler, I had personal business cards.) I would hand the cards to every Broadway professional I met and ask if I could email them any questions I had. It didn't work every time, but it did get me a few backstage tours. By the time I was ready to apply to colleges I already had a list of schools my mom and I had curated based on the top theatre programs in the country. My plan was to pick a school close to New York City so I had the best chance of meeting active professionals and could start working professionally while in college.

That plan was set aside when my dream of becoming an Imagineer at Disney became apparent my junior year of high school. My dream of becoming an Imagineer was the most challenging dream I had set for myself yet and, ultimately, it was the one that stuck.

 Director's Note:
Whatever your dream is, no matter how unattainable it seems, make a plan. There's no shame in failing to make your dream a reality—unless you never bother to try.

***

When I arrived in Orlando, I felt like I had made it. As I drove into the Walt Disney World Resort, passing under the iconic archways that line every road onto the property, I felt joy rush over me. It had been almost six years since I first saw "World of Color" in Disney's California Adventure. I couldn't believe that I was one *enormous* step closer to achieving the dream I had set out for just a few years prior. While I wasn't joining the company as an Imagineer, I knew there were few places better than Disney itself to work my way toward achieving that goal.

My first few months at Disney were interesting and full of unique highs and lows. I found it a challenge to be working on the front lines again after managing large venues and events. I had never worked on a team where I had to follow a Standard Operating Guide and didn't have the autonomy to be creative. This was also the first time I had ever worked on a team so large that I was scheduled by a trained skill and seniority level.

On the other hand, I was thrilled to be a part of delivering the magic. I absolutely loved the cast and shows I was a part of, surrounded by people with similar interests as me. I had never had such an easy time making friends before in my life, and every waking moment I wasn't working I was spending with my friends exploring the theme parks.

After the first few months, I started to enjoy my new way of life. I appreciated having a relatively set schedule from week to week. I liked the lack of surprises working in daily operations where every day was exactly the same, and eventually I even started to appreciate the lack of thought and creativity that went into my job. This honeymoon phase was mostly made possible by all of the excitement I had going on outside of work. For the first time in my adult life I actually had a social life. I was making up for the college years when I hadn't had the chance to really live because I was working too much.

This was all great while it lasted, but it wasn't long until my savings dried up and I started to get bored out of my mind at work. I was barely making enough money to cover rent and my car payment, and my ability to purchase groceries depended on how much overtime I was able to pick up each week. Luckily, I wasn't spending much money on anything else because with free admission to the theme parks as an employee, that's where my friends and I were spending all of our time. Another unplanned financial move that helped me out was living three miles from work and driving a Honda Civic, so I only had to fill up with gas once every two to three weeks. To cover my growing financial problems, I started to look for side jobs and connect with the local bar owners to offer AV support like I had in Philly.

With my financial problems temporarily under control, I started to talk to my leadership about my boredom. I still enjoyed working on the shows, but after six months of pushing set pieces and running audio for eight to ten shows per day, I started to feel as though my brain was rotting. I couldn't remember the last time I had to think for myself or make a quick decision to keep a production on the air. I needed to feel challenged again in order to stay motivated. Unfortunately, due to the timing of my request, there wasn't much advice my leadership could offer other than to continue to be patient.

As the year went on, I picked up contracts outside of work here and there. Overtime was sparse during the slower months, and occasionally I wasn't able to pay the balance on my credit card (something I ALWAYS do). By the time the holidays rolled around, I was really starting to get frustrated at work and my student loans were no longer in deferment, causing my financial problems to spin out of control. I was starting to lose sleep, which made me less fun to work with and soon led to negative feedback at work about being tired and grumpy. This is when I started to question whether I had made the right decision to leave my career in sports to chase my dream of working at Disney.

I felt like I was trying everything I could to network with other departments in the company in order to find a position that would better fit my skills—and hopefully would pay more—but I kept getting a lot of the same answers.

"Put your time in, you'll get there."

"Everything here goes slowly. You just have to be patient."

"Keep your head low and your time will come."

I appreciated all of the advice that my coworkers and leaders from other departments were providing, but I was running out of options. Financially I didn't think I could make it to the one-year mark without being in a ton of credit card debt. On the career front I had respect for the team and organization I was part of, but I had growing concerns about how it would look on my resume. In the years leading up to Disney I had managed venues and events for tens of thousands of fans, built, hired, and trained teams of professionals, and managed event budgets worth half a million dollars. Now I was spending six days per week running the same four microphones for a twenty-eight-minute show with a canned soundtrack.

One afternoon I received a call from a former coworker of mine, a technical director I worked for in Philadelphia during college.

"Hey Brett, how's Disney?" he asked, sounding more chipper than usual.

"Magical," I answered sarcastically.

"Ha! Well your name just came up in a meeting. Sarah just took over as the Vice President of Operations for the new stadium, and she's looking for a technical director to manage the venue."

"Oh wow," I said as my mind started to race. I had a pretty good idea where this conversation was going.

"Yeah! So, she called to ask us if we had any recommendations, and your name was the first to come to mind. Do you think you would consider moving back up north?"

I was speechless. A year earlier I would have killed to be the technical director of an NFL stadium, but now taking it could mean giving up my dream.

"Yeah, that sounds amazing," I hesitantly responded. "I would definitely consider it."

 Blocking Note:
Another prime example of the power of a strong professional network and keeping in touch!

Being a referral, my interview process went very quickly. Within three days I had a video interview with the broadcast team, and later that same day human resources called me to discuss the salary range. Everything was moving so quickly that I didn't have any time to think. I started to call all of my mentors to get their input.

- There are only thirty NFL stadiums in the country. Am I an idiot if I give up this opportunity?
- I only started working at Disney eight months ago. Is it too soon to give up on my dream?
- If I leave in under a year, am I ever going to be offered a job with the company again?
- Am I going to regret my decision to leave Orlando when it's zero degrees in the northeast?
- If I take the position, am I just chasing the paycheck or title?
- Am I even qualified to run an NFL stadium?!

Needless to say, I didn't get much sleep that week. There wasn't any consistency in the advice I received from my parents and mentors. Some people told me I would be crazy to turn down the job managing the technology for one of the most well-known stadiums in the country. Other people recommended I give my dream of being an Imagineer more time. Even my parents were torn on the decision.

 Director's Note:
Reach out to those you trust for help before making any big career decisions. It's always helpful to talk through your thought process with someone else and get their input. For me, those people have always been my parents, my program director from college, and a few of my past bosses. The further removed the person is from your decision, the less biased they are, and the better insight they can provide.

To this day I believe this was the only career decision I've ever faced where there genuinely wasn't a right or wrong answer. Either way I would have been left asking myself *"what if"* and no matter what I chose, I'm sure I would have continued to lead a successful career.

The night before I had to make my final decision, I drove over to EPCOT to take a long walk around the park and think. EPCOT has always been my family's favorite Disney theme park. Its name is an acronym that stands for Experimental Prototype Community of Tomorrow. It was one of the last design projects that Walt worked on before he passed away in 1966. Walt Disney was far more than just an animator, director, and entertainer. He was a visionary and a futurist. Walt's dreams and aspirations went far beyond the world of film and themed entertainment. His idea for EPCOT was a prime example of what his dreams were for the future of our world.

Although Walt's original vision for EPCOT never came to be, the theme park that the Disney company built paid homage to Walt's visions of the future of science and technology. The park has changed many times over the years, and by the time you're reading this book the company will likely have just completed its largest renovation in the park's history. During the years I was there, the park was made up of two sections: Future World and The World Showcase. Along with a handful of rides and shows, Future World contained pavilions that showed off modern science and technology. The back of the park was (and should still be) The World Showcase, which was made of eleven countries surrounding the lake. Designed to be a permanent world's fair, each pavilion displays the architecture, culture, and food native to that country. To add to the authenticity, each country's pavilion was staffed by natives from that region.

As I walked around the park that night, I started to remember why I was there, why I had taken the leap. I thought back to the night my parents and I were standing around the lagoon in Disney's California Adventure waiting for "World of Color" to start, my sixteen-year-old self absolutely enamored by the technology on display and realizing on the downbeat of the opening number that I had found my calling. I thought about how I hadn't known a single person who worked for the Walt Disney Company and what I would have given for the opportunity to spend just ten minutes with someone who could give me advice on how to get my foot in the door.

I was that someone now. I worked for the Walt Disney Company. I got there. Sure, I hadn't achieved my ultimate dream of being an Imagineer, but I was a heck of a lot closer than I was six years ago. What would sixteen-year-old me say if he heard I was considering giving up on my dream after just eight months?

The following day I called the human resources team at the stadium and thanked them for the opportunity.

To put this decision into perspective, at the time, I was working in a department of close to 800 people where my seniority was so low that it would take twenty years until I could get my first Christmas or New Year's Day off. In my first year, I basically didn't have any say in what my days off were each week, so I usually would be scheduled to work six days with Wednesdays off. I got five paid days off per year, which I wasn't allowed to use yet because I hadn't been with the company more than nine months, and it would take me three years to start earning ten paid days off. If I had accepted the job with the stadium, I would have had a better title, moving expenses, PTO, a 401K, a flexible five-day schedule during the off season, and a six-figure salary.

Call me crazy, but after mulling over the decision for a few days, I never once regretted my choice. I knew that if I had moved back up north and started working full-time in sports again, the perfect opportunity to chase my dream may never have come. While the financial situation I was in was not ideal, I was twenty-three years old and didn't have to support anyone but myself. There would be no better time to continue taking that risk. At that point, I gave myself a five-year deadline. If I reached my fifth year with the company and still hadn't achieved my goal, I would leave. I was there to chase my dream of becoming an Imagineer. I knew it was a dream that would take a ton of work—and potentially more time than I was willing to wait—but it was worth a try.

SHOW NOTES:

- Whatever your dream is, no matter how unattainable it seems, make a plan. There's no shame in failing to make your dream a reality—unless you never bother to try.

- Reach out to those you trust before making any big career decisions. It's always helpful to talk through your thought process with someone else and get their input. For me, those people have always been my parents, my program director from college, and a few of my past bosses. The further removed the person is from your decision, the less biased they are, and the better insight they can provide.

- There is no better time than when you are young to take a risk. When you don't have anyone else to financially support, it is the best time to be selfish and chase your dreams. You have your entire career ahead of you to make money. Don't wait too long. You're not getting any younger.

Chapter 12:

Only You Know What's Best for You

Have you ever had a teacher or coach who told you that you couldn't do something? Maybe it was even your parent or a guidance counselor. How did you react to hearing this negative feedback from someone you perceived as a role model? Were you sad? Did you get angry? Did you feel like you were being misled? Or did you believe them?

We all need a role model, whether that role model is someone you're close to like a family member or teacher or someone you've never met like your favorite YouTuber or Michelle Obama. Having a role model helps you set targets and focus your vision of success. But it can be heartbreaking when your role model tells you something you don't want to hear. It can be even harder to tell whether their advice is actually good advice. The closer you are with that role model, the more you trust them, and the harder it is not to believe them. Sometimes you have to do just that though and decide for yourself what's right.

We've all been given bad advice at some point, and most of us have been given bad advice by someone we look up to. I've been lucky to have some amazing mentors and role models in my life, but I can't count the number of times I've been given really awful advice. After being disappointed enough times in my early career by leaders and people I looked up to, I've come to learn that **no one's advice should outweigh the decision you are feeling in your gut.** No one's. No one knows you better than you—not your friends, family, leaders, or coaches. (Only your dog knows you better than you.) Keeping this in mind, be open to advice, seek it, and get as many different perspectives as you can knowing, ultimately, only you know what's best for you. Don't let anyone else's opinion control your life.

***

Two years into my time in Orlando, life was going pretty well. Work was keeping me busy on events and projects that forced me out of my comfort zone and made me grow as a leader. In just a year I had gone from working on the same show six days a week to working on six different shows some days. From broadcasting events like Wheel of Fortune and The Chew to leading crews on complex installations, every day provided new challenges and experiences. While I hadn't yet achieved my formal goal of becoming an Imagineer, working on a wide variety of projects and events allowed me to expand my network across the company, which opened new opportunities. I had been called for a few interviews and was starting to receive some positive feedback on the skills I needed to improve.

Outside of work, my professional network around Orlando was starting to pay off. I spent my days off working as a freelancer for local hotels and convention centers. With Orlando being the most highly trafficked tourist destination in the world, tons of businesses hosted their conventions and summits at the resorts around town. Working on these events led to connections with major companies across the world, and it wasn't long until I was getting called to freelance in other cities.

During a night out over the holidays, a friend of mine asked about the conventions I was working on. She mentioned that she was on the opening team of the newly reimagined Planet Hollywood and that they were looking for a Technical Director. I told her I'd be happy to take a look at the project but was not looking for anything full-time.

Planet Hollywood is a chain of restaurants that opened up in the early 1990s. Originally launched in New York City, the concept was designed to be an entertainment dining experience that immersed guests in the world of film and television. With locations around the world from California to London, one of Planet Hollywood's largest locations is in Disney Springs in Orlando, Florida.

After agreeing to take a look at the project, I got a call from the general manager and went in to meet the team at their offices. It was clear from the start of the conversation that this was a big project and was going to take a lot of work. They described the vision for the newly imagined restaurant before sharing the renderings for the visual center-piece. Typically, Planet Hollywood restaurants are filled with famous movie memorabilia from Robert Earl's personal collection. The new concept for Orlando would still have the memorabilia but with the addition of a 160-degree, 4,000-square-foot, 4K video wall that surrounded the tables. My eyes lit up the second I saw the rendering.

At that point in my career, I had been the technical director and project manager for video broadcast installations worth tens of millions of dollars. I had hired, trained, and managed crews to operate those systems, and my resume and portfolio proved that. Unfortunately, all of that work happened away from Disney, so I was never able to prove myself to those whose attention I needed in order to land my true dream job in the company. Here was an opportunity to manage the installation, training, and turnover for a massive video system right in the middle of Disney's property. There could not have been a more perfect way to prove myself and capture the attention of the Imagineering team.

Blocking Note:

This example goes back to "Stepping Down in Rank to Step Up in Company." Just because I had proven my abilities on big projects for other companies doesn't mean that a massive organization like Disney would be willing to throw a big project my way. Everyone has to put their time in to prove themselves.

Director's Note:

Create a personal marketing plan. If you need to find a way to prove yourself to a prospective employer, think outside the box and search for opportunities that will get their attention.

A few days after our initial meeting, the general manager called and asked me to meet him at the restaurant for a tour of the construction site. When I arrived, he led me up the stairs, pointing out all of the new features and showing off the work that had been completed so far. His passion for the project was clear. He had been on the opening team of the restaurant over twenty years earlier when it first debuted, and he was thrilled to see his restaurant coming to life again.

As we walked through the main dining room, I looked up into the dome that would soon become the 4,000-square-foot projection screen. Even after working in professional stadiums and arenas much larger in scale, I was still amazed at the sheer size of the screen. I thought back to the first time I had seen large-scale projection mapping and how far the technology had come in just a few years.

We walked out to the back patio where a few of the executives were gathered. The general manager introduced me, we shook hands, then I was promptly bombarded with a barrage of questions varying from expected maintenance costs to depreciation value of the equipment, none of which I could provide any hard numbers for because I hadn't even been given the technical specifications yet. I must have done alright because the following day I got a call from human resources to start salary negotiations.

When I had started conversations with the team the week prior, I was under the impression that this would be a short-term contract or ongoing freelance engagement. Those assumptions did not match what the executives were thinking and over the following weeks I had a number of phone calls with them to discuss contractual options that would allow me to be a part-time contractor while still keeping my full-time job.

Most of the executives I spoke to could not understand why I wanted to stay full-time with Disney so badly. They tried to convince me that they could offer me a title, more money, room to grow my career without the corporate red tape, and the ability to travel to the other locations around the country. I have to commend them for really thinking outside the box and putting up a good fight. Under other circumstances I may have taken the offer to sign on with them full-time, but I knew where my passion was. After working in large-scale museums and restaurants for many years, I knew that it was simply going to be a learning experience and a great position to add to my resume, not the next big step in my career. Ultimately, we came to an agreement, and after receiving approval from both Disney and Planet Hollywood, I signed on as the Technical Director in a part-time contractor role.

Director's Note:

No matter what an employer says, there is always room for negotiation. While they may not be able to budge on the salary, there's always other ways to negotiate, such as a sign-on bonus, moving expenses, paid time off, or a flexible schedule and working location. Don't feel pressured into accepting a deal with a company. Only you know what's best for you, and you should fight for what your time, skill set, and experience is worth.

Blocking Note:

While at times they may not have been the most conventional company in the world, I cannot speak highly enough about the leadership and executives I worked with at Planet Hollywood and Earl Enterprises. They were always true to their word and genuinely cared about the well-being of their employees and staff.

After accepting the job as Technical Director at Planet Hollywood, my career at Disney started to get even more interesting. In the weeks leading up to the opening, I was in dozens of meetings with the Imagineering and Operations teams to discuss design and logistics. Those meetings led to invaluable new connections across the company, which ultimately led to future interviews with Imagineering.

On the other hand, the team I was part of viewed my involvement in the project with mixed feelings. Some of my coworkers and leaders were supportive of the experience while others were opposed to me moonlighting with another company. This led to some contention and drama that had to be dealt with. Almost every single one of my coworkers and leaders had second jobs with other theme parks or venues around town. Having multiple jobs was almost a necessity in order to live in Orlando with how little we were being paid. While I tried to ignore the negative feedback, there were certain times when I had to defend myself by outlining that there wasn't any difference between me freelancing with a local restaurant and someone having a second job at a competing theme park.

While I shouldn't have had to care what others thought about my freelance work, there were a number of weeks when I was getting called into five or six meetings to be questioned about my position. Ultimately, I had the approval and it was none of my coworkers' business what I did with my time after I clocked out.

 Director's Note:
Leave the drama at the stage door. Unfortunately, drama is often part of life. It is very rare to come across a team that has absolutely zero drama. When you are the focus of the drama, it can reflect poorly on you and your performance. While it's really frustrating to deal with and often terrifying to confront, it's best to approach the problem head-on and take care of it before it spirals out of control.

Aside from the people who were just causing drama, there were others who did not understand why I was choosing to be involved in the project.

"Why are you working for a restaurant?"

"Disney won't care what you're doing for them."

"How's that going to improve your resume?"

"Their technology is junk compared to what we're using!"

I heard it all. While some of it may have been cynicism or jealousy, most of it was just simple inexperience.

Most people don't think outside the box when planning their next career step. They get stuck believing that if they just put their time in, an opportunity will be magically handed to them. While that may be the case for a lucky few, that plan will not work for everybody. After three years of being surrounded by people who had been stuck for over fifteen years, still hanging on to the hope that their time would come, I knew that I was not going to put my career and financial well-being in jeopardy by waiting around. I was going to have to find other avenues to gain experience and prove myself.

 Director's Note:
If your current position doesn't offer you the experience or opportunities necessary to learn and grow, look for other channels outside of your full-time work to gain that experience. This can be through higher education or certification programs, shadowing or volunteering, freelancing, or picking up a part-time job on nights and weekends.

No matter what my leaders or coworkers had to say, I knew what was best for me. I knew that I needed to gain more experience as a technical director and find ways to prove my abilities. While Planet Hollywood may have been a restaurant instead of a theme park or performance venue, it was a perfectly viable channel to gain that experience and it was tied closely enough to the Disney community that my impact could be seen by those whose attention I needed.

Fast-forward a few years after accepting the position with Planet Hollywood. In interviews with two separate Silicon Valley tech companies, I have been asked more questions about my short time with Planet Hollywood than about my four years with the Walt Disney Company. Although it was a smaller, lesser-known company, the title and experience were more attractive to the big tech giants than those of the various positions I held with Disney.

Only you know what's best for you.

 ## SHOW NOTES:

- No one's advice should outweigh your gut feeling. Only you know what's best for you

- Always have an escape route. Relying on a single job as your sole source of income leaves you one step away from financial stress in the event you lose that job. Having a paying side gig or part-time job can greatly decrease the chances that you'll be completely without a paycheck should you lose your job, and it could be the temporary escape route you need while you secure your next step.

- Create a personal marketing plan. If you need to find a way to prove yourself to a prospective employer, think outside the box and search for opportunities that will get their attention.

- There is always room for negotiation. While an employer may not be able to budge on the salary, there's always other ways to negotiate, such as a sign-on bonus, moving expenses, paid time off, or a flexible schedule and working location. Don't feel pressured into accepting a deal with a company. Only you know what's best for you, and you should fight for what your time, skill set, and experience is worth.

- Leave the drama at the stage door. When you are the focus of the drama, it can reflect poorly on you and your performance. While it's really frustrating to deal with and often terrifying to confront, it's best to approach the problem head-on and take care of it before it spirals out of control.
- You don't have to rely solely on your current job for development and growth opportunities. Look for other channels outside of work to gain experience on your own. This can be through higher education or certification programs, shadowing or volunteering, freelancing, or picking up a part-time job on nights and weekends.

Chapter 13:

Don't Fight the Writing on the Wall

As I mentioned before, it's very rare to come across someone whose career was a straight line. Today, it's more common than ever to change roles, companies, or even careers many times before you find what you really love to do. There's no shame in finding that what you thought you would love to do is not what you expected. Every experience is a great learning opportunity, even if it's just learning what you don't want to do. Aside from the educational aspects, every job grows your professional network and can lead to connections for future opportunities.

Sometimes the problem isn't that you're not enjoying the job or company; it's that the opportunity to grow just isn't there. Personally, I find this to be one of the most frustrating career experiences and, unfortunately, it's just part of the journey. It may be that you've topped out in your current role but there aren't any open positions at the next level. In other cases, there may be positions open that could help you advance in your career but don't lead down the career path you would like to take. Finally, there are situations where you are stuck in a company that expects you to put your career goals on hold in order to match their timeline. That is not a healthy work relationship.

A job is a partnership between you and your employer. They should be investing in your growth and development just as much as you are investing in theirs. If you are part of a team or company that views you as just another cog in the wheel, odds are they do not care much about your career development or future with the company. Keep in mind your leverage in these situations. Even employers who feel that their employees are expendable are aware of the cost of interviewing, onboarding, and training someone new if you choose to leave.

It can cost a company tens of thousands of dollars just to interview, hire, and onboard an employee—and that's before even paying a cent of the employee's salary. Once an employee has been with the company for an extended period of time, the value of that employee goes up because of training costs and historical knowledge. Whether you're a vice president or third-shift maintenance employee, it will take time and money to replace you and your experience.

Unfortunately, many professionals will be faced with the decision of how long to keep waiting for an opportunity to arise with their current employer before deciding to leave the company. While everyone's situation is different, personally I have found that being forthcoming with my leadership about my career trajectory and planned timeline is the best approach to finding growth opportunities within a company. Eventually though, there may be a point where the opportunity to grow just simply isn't there and you may have to make the tough choice to leave.

***

By my fourth year at Disney, I had built the strongest intercompany professional network of my career. I had worked in all four parks, been on the opening team of two new lands, a multi-use sports arena and half a dozen shows, and had worked on more than a hundred events and broadcasts. I had cultivated relationships with departments on every end of property, from Imagineering and IT to Park Operations and Facilities Management.

Although I had a ton of amazing experiences and the opportunity to be a part of countless teams, my career growth was still being held back by the position I was in. One week I would be coordinating the engineering for a live national broadcast and the next I would be taping cables to the carpet and driving a forklift on third shift.

Outside of work, I was being hired by companies across the country as a broadcast engineer and project manager for multi-million-dollar corporate keynotes. I was living a double life, and it was getting more frustrating to manage by the week. It felt morally degrading to go from a two-week show managing a crew of eighty union technicians in a convention center to being told that I needed to clock in and out for lunch within the allotted thirty minutes or I would receive a point on my record card. It was like being a college student with a curfew. I could live on my own, but still had to be home by 10 p.m.

To make matters even more frustrating, I was making more money outside of work freelancing in a single night than I was making in an entire week at my full-time job. The only reason I was still hanging on was because I was determined to achieve my goal of making it to Imagineering. But I was getting close to my five-year limit, and the odds weren't looking good for me achieving my goal.

 Blocking Note:

Everyone's situation is different. I have dozens of friends who have led amazingly successful careers at Disney and in the wider theme park industry. Many of them listened to the advice they were given by their leadership and continued to put their time in. Some spent five to ten years on the front lines before working their way into management and up the corporate ladder while others managed to land a position on the design teams or Imagineering straight out of college or within their first few years. Personally, I believe the timing simply wasn't right for me, and I was not willing to keep my career on hold any longer. You have to do what's best for you.

For months I sent weekly emails asking for meet-and-greets and one-on-ones with different departments. Every morning I would browse the internal job boards and apply to any job that seemed interesting. After six months, I had been to more than fifteen interviews, forty meetings, and had exchanged over 200 emails with professionals across the company. In the meantime, I was turning down interview opportunities from competitors and watching coworkers who I trained as interns get promoted around me. I was nearing the point of quitting when I got an email a week before my birthday from one of the project managers asking me to meet with him to discuss a project.

This was a project manager I had exchanged emails with a handful of times over the years for various projects but had never had the chance to meet with one-on-one. He was a decision-maker who usually had a lot of say when it came to staffing projects. The week leading up to the meeting, I drove myself nuts racking my brain about what he wanted to talk about. Was there a new project that he wanted me on? Was this finally an opportunity to take the next step in my career? Is there a big announcement I haven't gotten word of yet?

The day of the meeting, I arrived outside of his office fifteen minutes early with paperwork for all of the projects I was working on at the time. I had a list of questions for him in case he asked if I had any and some notes jotted down on a piece of paper tucked into the clear pocket of my binder. I was nervous but ecstatic. This was the project manager I had looked up to for the past few years. He had reached out to set up the meeting. This could be the start of the next big step in my career—and it was all happening on my birthday.

After I sat down in his office, he asked how my projects were going and if I had any concerns about the upcoming event season. We chatted for a bit about the big project my team had just completed and some of the challenges we were facing during the close-out phase. Finally, the conversation started to shift toward upcoming projects as he began to discuss the staffing plans for the big shows in the pipeline. He went on to share who would be managing the projects before he asked what my goals were. I told him I wanted to be a technical director like I was doing for projects outside of the company.

"Huh," he looked at me, surprised. "What relevant experience do you feel you have?"

I looked at him shocked. He already knew what I had been working on the past few years, both inside and outside of the company.

"Well, I just completed the venue build, the restaurant on the east side of the property, and the four corporate keynotes at the convention center. Prior to moving down here I managed the opening of an arena and spent four years working in broadcasting for an NFL team," I replied, a little dumbstruck.

"Look, Brett," he responded slowly, as if to emphasize the seriousness behind his answer. "I don't care what you do outside of here. We promote from within. You need to prove yourself to our team."

My face went white with defeat, "What about the work that I just completed for the opening of the new venue?"

He smiled as he responded, "Yeah, you were a technician. Being a technical director takes a lot more work than that."

My face transformed from white to deep red with anger, "I worked over eighty-five hours a week from Thanksgiving to New Year's to get that venue open on time. I scheduled and coordinated over 300 scheduling blocks. I met daily with a dozen vendors and contractors to align scope and schedules, handled all executive communications, and received a personal thank you from the vice presidents of two separate departments outlining how my work played a crucial role in the success of the project."

"Brett, look," he replied calmly with just a hint of sass. "You're a technician, not a technical director. If you would like to gain the experience to be a technical director, I recommend you take another ten to fifteen years to work as a technician in the parks, leave the company for a few years and come back, then we'll talk."

I didn't have a response to his comment. I grabbed my binder and left.

As I stormed out of his office, I ran into an intern I had trained in park operations a few years earlier. She had just graduated with an arts degree in acting when she started with the department as an intern.

"Hey, what are you doing here?" I tried to hide my frustration as I greeted her.

"Hey! I was just assigned as the technical director for the new show!" She could barely contain her excitement.

I walked out without replying to her.

That night while out at the bowling alley with my friends for my birthday, I told them I was done. After dozens of interviews, hundreds of emails, and four years of watching less experienced people get promoted around me, I had officially seen the writing on the wall. It was time to leave.

I wasn't angry. I was just sad. It was no one's fault—not mine, not the project manager's, and not the company's. Life is a game of politics. It's all about who you know and a little bit of being in the right place at the right time. If I had continued to keep a positive attitude and work hard for the following few years, I'm sure an opportunity would have eventually come. However, I knew that there were better opportunities out there, and Disney would always be there. I could either keep working in my existing role at Disney and gain the necessary experience outside of work, or I could find an alternative route.

 ## SHOW NOTES:

- Sometimes the opportunity to grow your career is not an option in your current position. Whether it's because you've topped out in your role, there aren't any available positions at the next level, or your employer isn't providing opportunities for your growth, when you come to this conclusion, you have to decide what the best next step is for you.
- Set a time limit. Life is too short to wait around hoping that an opportunity will come. Decide how long you are willing to wait for an opportunity to be presented before you have to seek opportunities elsewhere. Sometimes leaving or just mentioning that you're considering it is just enough to get opportunities moving.
- You know exactly what you are capable of. Never let anyone else, no matter their experience, position, or title, belittle your abilities.
- As frustrated, sad, or angry as you may be after being passed over for a position, keep a level head. Remember, NEVER BURN ANY BRIDGES.

Chapter 14:
LinkedIn Unleashes Its True Powers

U p to this point, I've shared quite a few examples of how I used LinkedIn as a tool to develop my career. I've used it for researching connections to employers I was trying to get in touch with. I've used it as a networking tool to build new connections. I've used it to apply to jobs, and I've used it to search for candidates myself. Of all of the ways LinkedIn has helped me grow my professional network and career, I will always remember the first time it unleashed its true powers, playing a key role in the path to where I am today.

In the months following my decision to leave Disney, I spent a lot of time soul-searching. I met with my mentors from over the years, discussed ideas with my parents, and reached out to my former bosses for advice. Deciding which direction to take my career was a hard decision. For the prior nine years, my end goal was always to make it to Imagineering. While on that journey, I had spent time working in professional sports, broadcasting, theatre, events, and dozens of freelance positions, but I never viewed any of them as the *end goal*. While most of those positions and opportunities were fun, none of them checked all of my boxes.

This job search was a unique one because the employer I was looking to leave was the same employer I was hoping to gain enough experience to get the attention of again in the future. My plan was to find a job that would help me grow my skills and professional network while still enjoying all of the other aspects of my life and career that are important to me.

When considering a career move, I use a checklist of items that are important to me to decide if it is a good move. It's a system of checks and balances to make sure that I am chasing the position for the right reasons as opposed to simply chasing a title, money, or change. The checklist is best organized in a Venn diagram:

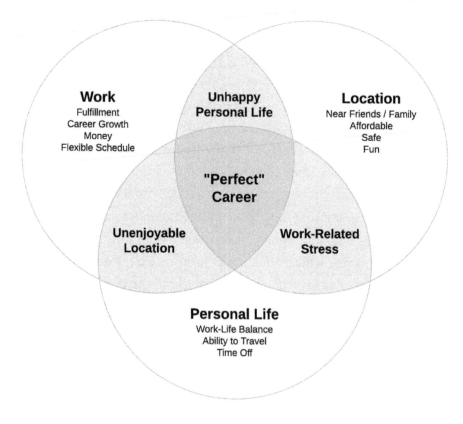

Considerations in the Work category:

- **Fulfillment:** Will my daily job make me feel like I am leading a fulfilling career?
- **Career Growth:** Will the position help me grow my career? Is there room for growth in the company?
- **Money:** Does the job adequately pay me for my experience and position? Does it meet my financial needs for daily life, future savings goals, and retirement planning?
- **Flexible Schedule:** Does the job offer a flexible schedule or working hours that I will enjoy?

Considerations in the Location category:

- **Near Friends and Family:** Will the job allow me to live in an area that is close to my friends and family or offer remote working options that let me visit often?
- **Affordable:** Is the job located in an affordable area? Will I be able to afford a house or an apartment? Will I have to have roommates in order to make ends meet? What is the tax structure in the state I will be a resident of?
- **Safe:** Is the area I will be living and working in safe?
- **Fun:** What is there to do in the area? Is it in or close to a major city or is it in the middle of nowhere? What's the average age group of the area? Am I going to be able to easily meet new people and make friends?

Considerations in the Personal Life category:

- **Work–Life Balance:** Will the job allow for a work–life balance that I enjoy?
- **Ability to Travel:** Will I have the time off and financial means to travel? Will I be able to secure time off far enough in

advance to be able to plan a trip? Will I be expected to be on call for emergencies at work while traveling?

- **Time Off:** What does time off look like in the job or industry? Will I be working six to seven days per week with extended periods of time off during a slow season or will I be working a standard five-day schedule? How much paid time off do I get and how soon after starting can I use it? Are time off requests based on seniority or how are requests reviewed and approved?

Director's Note:

Decide what factors are most important to you when considering accepting a new job. Write them down while you have a clear mind so that they are readily available to review when weighing your options.

There are a lot of factors I consider when thinking about accepting a new position. For some of you, those factors may sound a little odd, like time off requests based on seniority and working six to seven days per week with extended time off during a slow season. After working in theme parks and live entertainment for over a decade, these are just common parts of my life. When opening a new show or venue, it is common to work seven days per week until the project is complete followed by some extra time off to recover. As crazy as this sounds, some people actually prefer this type of schedule, which makes it an important factor to consider.

Personally, prior to starting at Google, I can't remember a time in my adult life when I worked a standard Monday through Friday, 9 a.m.–5 p.m. job. Even in high school I was working nights, weekends, and holidays. By the time I got to my fourth year in Orlando, I dreamed of having even a single day of the *weekend* off. *Weekends* in the entertainment and theme park industry are irrelevant. *Weekends* are not Saturdays and Sundays; *weekends* are whenever you have off. For most Broadway professionals, weekends are Sunday nights and Mondays. On tour, weekends can be the travel time between cities or occasional dark days between performances. In major theme parks like Disney and Universal, weekends are whenever you manage to get a day off.

The craziest thing about working on that type of schedule for so many years was that when I finally landed myself in a position that had the same schedule every week Monday through Friday, 9 a.m.–5 p.m., with Saturdays, Sundays, and holidays off, I was so bored I didn't know what to do with all of my spare time. That's what led me to adding a *flexible schedule* as a factor to consider in the work category. Sometimes I enjoy having an occasional Wednesday morning off to get chores done or go grocery shopping while avoiding crowds. On the flip side, sometimes I would rather be working on a Sunday afternoon instead of lounging around the house. Your preferences are completely up to you. You have to decide which factors to consider and which ones are most important to you when considering a new position.

 Director's Note:
Take some time to think about what schedule and working environment you thrive in most. In today's quickly advancing age of remote and hybrid work, negotiating for a schedule and working environment that fits you best might be terms that your prospective employer is open to discussing.

After months of looking around and having a few interviews with professional sports teams and theatres, I was still undecided about what I wanted for my next career move. The thought of leaving Disney was eating away at me from the inside. Even though I wasn't making enough money to afford my own place, my schedule didn't allow me to see my family on most holidays, and my career was in a holding pattern, the life that I had was the best four years of my life up until that point. I had friends and coworkers who were indistinguishable from family, the Disney community was my home, and I absolutely loved being a part of bringing the magic of Disney to life.

But I knew I had to make a change. If I stayed where I was, there wasn't any guarantee that I would ever meet my career goals, it would have taken me until my late thirties to be able to pay off my student loans and possibly afford a small house, and I may never have had the money to retire.

In late 2018, after months of soul-searching and meeting with prospective employers, I was hired by a Seattle-based production company for a large corporate keynote that was scheduled to take place in Orlando. The event was a week-long convention that hosted more than 40,000 leaders from the broader tech industry. Due to the size and visibility of the event, the production company that produced the broadcast hired local engineers as subject matter experts to be onsite readily available for the duration of the event in case anything went wrong. As one of those engineers, I was able to set my own rate and negotiate my hours. I received approval to take time off from my other jobs to dedicate a full two weeks to being onsite for the event.

From pulling control fiber lines and focusing projectors to managing the production crews and handling logistics with the local streaming providers, it was a jam-packed two weeks of long hours and endless curveballs. The crew installing and running the event was made up of more than 280 production professionals from around the United States along with a few hundred local union stagehands, carpenters, and teamsters. This made for organized chaos—and some amazing networking opportunities.

By the time the event ended, I had already been asked by the executive producer to submit a quote for traveling out to Dallas and Las

Vegas for two upcoming conventions. For the first time, I was actually considering quitting my job and going freelance. But freelancing was a terrifying idea.

Freelancing in any industry has its pros and cons. The freedom to set your own schedule and rates can be great. You can choose the way you live your life without being tied to an employer's pay and schedule. On the other hand, depending on work continuing to come in and chasing down clients for checks on top of not having health insurance is enough to keep most people returning to their cubicle every Monday morning.

I was a freelancer for most of college. Personally, I enjoyed the flexibility and the variety of work from day to day, but even in college with low financial needs and being covered by my parents' medical insurance, some months were tight! Thankfully, once I landed my first full-time job, I didn't have to drop all of my freelance work. Depending on your weekly work schedule and whether or not you have to sign a non-compete agreement with your employer, you may be able to keep up occasional freelance work while continuing to work full-time. I had a lot of coworkers in Orlando who did just that. They were hourly, full-time, or seasonal with the theme parks and spent the rest of their time freelancing. This allowed them to obtain insurance through work along with a base pay that would cover their necessities and take away the stress of waiting for the paychecks from clients when they freelanced.

When I returned to work the week after the convention, I told my boss about the experience. He had been giving me advice on my career journey for almost a year at that point and coming from a similar background, he knew quite a bit about the production industry. He immediately latched on to the idea and began helping me build a plan to kick up my freelance work as a broadcast consultant while continuing to keep my full-time job. We discussed how we could make the schedule work and who I could hire to help backfill me when I could not get off work. Our discussions quickly led to developing a vision of the target market for my services and marketing plans to grow my business. Plans were rolling quickly, and I was beginning to get really excited about the possibilities of advancing my career while continuing to keep my foot in the door just enough to keep focused on my end goal.

After weeks of planning and preparing to kick off the business, I received a message one slow afternoon in February that would change the course of my career. It was a less enjoyable day at work. I was out on the loading dock with a few of my coworkers unpacking pallets of display monitors for a project I was managing. Having just finished managing a multi-million-dollar keynote followed by the NFL ProBowl broadcast, I was less than enthusiastic about spending a week unloading trucks and breaking down pallets because the low-budget project I was managing did not allow me to hire any help. Of course, being February in Orlando, it was still 85 degrees with 99 percent humidity, so even at 10 a.m. the sweat was dripping down my face. During our first fifteen-minute break of the morning, the crew headed into the building to grab coffee while I stayed out on the loading dock to check my email.

I leaned over the guardrail at the edge of the dock peering down at my phone. Following my usual routine, I started with my email, scrolling through the messages to check for anything time-sensitive before moving on to Facebook and Instagram. After a few minutes of failing to catch the dopamine rush we're all subconsciously looking for when scrolling endlessly through social media, I opened up the LinkedIn app. There were a few notifications about job postings, some updates from people I was connected to, and a few messages. The first two messages were the usual spam but the third was a personal message from a name that didn't sound familiar.

From: Angelica Houston
Subject: Unique Opportunity with Google!

Before opening the message, I assumed that it was either spam or just a lead to signing up for a new Google service. But I opened up the message.

Hi Brett,

My name is Angelica and I work for the Staffing team here at Google. I came across your LinkedIn page and think your background could be a great asset to Google's Experience Studio Team.

Google is looking for innovative people who not only have strong technical ability, but can also design, develop and maintain a portfolio of Google's Experience Studio's physical spaces and interactive exhibits. You will have the opportunity to drive complex projects that bring Google's magic to life.

Given your expertise in technical integration, project management and troubleshooting experience, an opportunity as such would be a great fit for you.

Please let me know if you are interested in learning more.

My first reaction to reading the message was sheer confusion. Why in the world would Google be looking for a technical entertainment professional with a background in managing live events and broadcasts? This was quickly followed with a flood of images from the Owen Wilson and Vince Vaugh movie where they applied to be interns at Google. I could not wrap my head around what a day-to-day job would be like working in a major tech company. I just pictured myself sitting in a cubicle staring at CAD drawings all day and responding to emails. Believe it or not, I actually didn't immediately respond to the message.

Later that day, I showed the message to my boss. His eyes lit up with excitement.

"Dude, this is the break you've been looking for!" (Yes, my former boss called me dude.) "Just imagine the opportunities that this will lead to!"

I stared back at him, understanding what he was saying but almost not wanting to hear him, "Yeah, but it's corporate. What do they need someone with my skills for? I don't want to be running keynotes and town halls all day."

My boss looked back at me, already prepared with a rebuttal.

"Whether that is the case or not, you have been looking for a way to advance your career since I met you two years ago. You have hit roadblock after roadblock, none of which you have had any control over. You've admitted more than once that you've seen the writing on the wall. The only way that you're going to achieve your dreams in this company is by hanging on for another twenty years hoping for the right people to retire or die. Or you can leave the company, gain some incredible experience elsewhere, build a name for yourself, then have this company recruit you just like Google is doing right now. You have one of the largest, most sought-after employers on the planet seeking you out right now. Are you really going to turn down that kind of opportunity?"

He was right.

I replied to Angelica's message and over the next two months went through one of the most intense interview processes offered by any company around the world. After screenings, video interviews, being flown to their New York City campus, more paperwork and phone interviews, in April 2019, I was offered a job at Google.

So why is this chapter titled *LinkedIn Unleashes Its True Powers*? At the time the recruiter reached out to me, I did not have a single first-degree connection with anyone who worked for Alphabet, Google, or any of its *Other Bets*. In fact, I only had a single second-degree connection with someone who worked for the company, and they were a former vendor who only worked on a project remotely with the company for three months. Even with my best networking efforts, I wasn't able to get in touch with anyone who was connected to the company to provide advice during the interview process.

So how did the recruiter find me?

The recruiter found me based on the keywords and experience listed in my profile. Recruiters on LinkedIn have powerful tools that allow them to search for candidates based on any criteria they choose. LinkedIn will even algorithmically rank the candidates, displaying the strongest potential candidates first and highlighting the criteria they best match. My profile showed up in the recruiter's search results because of the combination of AV and project management skills I had listed.

The lesson here? Always keep your LinkedIn profile up-to-date, even if you aren't actively searching for a job.

Director's Note:

If you want to see how your profile ranks compared to other professionals in your industry, sign up for a trial of LinkedIn Premium and visit the careers section. You will have access to tools that show you how your profile looks to recruiters and ways to improve your ranking in search results.

Show Notes:

- Decide what factors are most important to you when considering accepting a new job. Write them down while you have a clear mind so that they are readily available to review when weighing your options.

- Take some time to think about what schedule and working environment you thrive in most. In today's quickly advancing age of remote and hybrid work, negotiating for a schedule and working environment that fits you best might be terms that your prospective employer is open to discussing.
- If you're thinking about starting to pick up freelance or consulting work, but you aren't ready to totally take the plunge and quit your job, talk to your employer about their non-compete policies. If you are freelancing in a completely different industry than the one you are working in, odds are your employer can't prohibit it as long as it doesn't affect your availability and concentration at work. If they are open to the idea but you're concerned about the schedule, talk to your employer about ways to flex your schedule. Outline the opportunity to your employer as a way for you to develop and diversify skills outside of work, which in turn makes you a more valuable asset to the company.
- Always keep your LinkedIn profile up-to-date, even when you aren't actively searching for a job.
- Seek ways to improve your LinkedIn profile by adding skills, improving the description details of your work, requesting referrals from your notable connections, and comparing your profile to other professionals in your industry.

Chapter 15:

The Importance of a Strong Professional Network

I n 2020, I had the pleasure of speaking with dozens of students and young professionals seeking career advice. Coming from all backgrounds, ages, and demographics, the people I speak with are different in many ways, but they all have at least one thing in common: They were driven enough to take initiative and ask for help.

These career conversations really started to pick up in early 2020 amid the global pandemic, which made for a very interesting change in narrative. In the few years leading up to the pandemic, the job market was doing well and there were often more open positions than there were candidates, which made it a candidate's market. In early 2020, jobless claims hit the highest numbers in decades and suddenly with millions of people out of work, it became an employer's market. These changes made career conversations very interesting.

At the beginning of the pandemic, almost no one was hiring. Businesses were shutting down on a daily basis, every company was announcing furloughs and layoffs, and even the businesses still thriving had hiring freezes. At that time, most of the conversations were focused on how to make use of the free time at home to better the chances of employment once companies started hiring again. The recommendation I provided to everyone, no matter where they were in their education or career, was to take online classes and certification courses. This would continue to grow their marketable skills while keeping their brains sharp instead of endless hours of swiping through social media or watching streaming services.

There are endless resources online for continuing to educate yourself, and you don't have to be in a global pandemic to take advantage of them.

*Current as of December 2020

- LinkedIn Learning
- YouTube & YouTube Learning - **Free!**
- Udemy
- Khan Academy
- Coursera
- iTunesU - **Free!**
- Podcasts - **Free!**
- Stanford Online
- Harvard Extension - **Free!**
- Open Yale Courses
- MIT OpenCourseWare - **Free!**
- Carnegie Mellon Open Learning Initiative
- Codeacademy
- TED-Ed - **Free!**
- Masterclass

... and the list goes on.

Most of the people I spoke to early in the pandemic were out of work or were students whose internships were cancelled due to the pandemic. Most of them shared a similar concern: "How is having a gap in my work history going to look on my resume?"

My answer to this question every time was simply that any employer will understand a candidate who has a gap in their job history in 2020. Similar to 2008, it will come as no surprise to any employer to hear that you lost your job and were not immediately able to find another one. When recruiters and hiring managers see that gap on your resume in the future, the question that I firmly believe they will all be asking is:

"What did you do to better yourself while stuck at home in 2020?"

I shouldn't have to tell you that a recruiter or hiring manager isn't going to want to hear the following answers to that question:

- *"I watched way too much Netflix and Hulu."*
- *"I gained the quarantine fifteen."*
- *"I sat around stressed watching the news."*
- *"I don't know."*

What recruiters and hiring managers are going to want to hear you spent your time doing might include:

- *"I took courses online."*
- *"I attended virtual trainings and seminars."*
- *"I earned a certification in a certain subject."*
- *"I read a lot of great books I had been wanting to catch up on."*
- *"I worked on updating my resume."*
- *"I started an online business."*
- *"I freelanced."*

- *"I applied to jobs."*
- *"I reached out to professionals on LinkedIn for advice."*
- *"I worked on growing my professional network."*

... and the list goes on. The moral of the story is whether it's a global pandemic, economic recession, or a career dry spell, don't focus on what you can't control. Concentrate on what you can control: continuing your education, bettering yourself, and growing your professional network.

As 2020 continued, many employers started posting jobs again and the career conversations I was having shifted from self-development to how to market yourself, how to stand out to employers, and how to land interviews. This is where the great divide between the two types of people I met with started to become apparent.

As I mentioned at the start of the chapter, everyone who took the time to meet with me was at least driven enough to take the time to reach out for advice. That was a fantastic first step for many of them; however, for at least half of them, that drive didn't extend to their applications. This isn't to say they were less driven than the other half; they were just never taught how to *properly* apply for a job.

What do I mean by *properly* apply for a job?

Roughly half of the people I was meeting with were getting calls for interviews. Regardless of whether they got called back for follow-up interviews or were offered the position, they were at least getting a call from the employer they applied to. The other half weren't even getting called for initial screenings.

After reviewing everyone's LinkedIn profiles, cover letters, and resumes, the first three questions I asked were:

- *"How many positions have you applied for?"*
- *"What platforms did you use to apply?"*
- *"Who have you spoken to at the company?"*

This is where the divide became apparent between those who knew how to *properly* apply to jobs and those who did not.

General answers from those *NOT* getting called for interviews:

- *"How many positions have you applied for?"*
  - *A: 3–5*
- *"What platforms did you use to apply?"*
  - *A: LinkedIn, Indeed, various job boards*
- *"Who have you spoken to at the company?"*
  - *A: No one. I don't know anyone at the company.*

General answers from those getting called for interviews:

- *"How many positions have you applied for?"*
  - *A: 10–20*
- *"What platforms did you use to apply?"*
  - *A: LinkedIn, company website, other job platforms*
- *"Who have you spoken to at the company?"*
  - *A: A few past / current employees, a recruiter on LinkedIn, and a personal connection*

Now I'd bet some of you are immediately thinking, *"Well it's not their fault they don't know anyone at the company!"* or *"Of course the one group is getting called for interviews if they have inside connections, but not everyone is fortunate enough to have those connections!"*

Let's take a quick step back to Chapter 6. Did I know a single person in the sports industry when I was looking for internships with the Philadelphia Phillies? Nope. In fact, I didn't even have a second-degree connection, and I wasn't able to get a response from the producer after two follow-up emails. And what did I do? I widened my search to include all

Philadelphia Sports teams and found a second-degree connection with the Philadelphia Eagles and asked for an introduction. Ten years later, my connections to sports teams have grown from a single second-degree connection with one NFL team to first-degree connections with almost every MLB, NHL, and NFL team in the United States.

What about in high school when I decided I wanted to work for Disney and I didn't have any connections to the company? LinkedIn was only a few years old and I didn't even have an account yet. I asked my friends, family, school, and professional connections for almost a year before I made my first contact, and it was almost another year after that that I made the connection who ultimately referred me.

I guarantee, no matter what company or industry you are looking to get into, no matter where you are in your education or career, and no matter how big or small your network is, you have the ability to get in touch with somebody who can get you connected.

Here are a few ideas:

- LinkedIn
  - Search for first- and second-degree connections, ask for introductions
  - Go to the company's page and check for employees who may have gone to the same school as you or have had a similar job history
  - Sign up for LinkedIn Premium and unlock the ability to message third-degree connections *Be careful with this option. I'd recommend limiting your messages to recruiters. I don't recommend dropping your name with the VP or CEO.*
- Friends and family
  - Ask around and put the word out on social media *Don't do this publicly if you're concerned about your current employer seeing that you're searching for jobs.*

- College Alumni Network
  - Reach out to your university's alumni network to see if there are any alumni who work for the company you are trying to get in touch with.

Below are a few more ideas that I don't personally recommend but have been known to work occasionally:

- Reach out to the company on social media.
- Stop by their office to apply in person and ask to chat with someone.
- Mail a professionally printed copy of your portfolio and resume addressed directly to the hiring manager or recruiter you are trying to get in touch with.

So why is it so important to find a connection to the company or industry you are applying to anyway? Among the endless reasons why this is important, I find the following three to be the most crucial.

Avoid having your resume auto-rejected

It's crazy to me that this is not taught in school these days, but did you know that it's possible for your application to be auto-deleted by computer software before it ever even makes it to a recruiter or hiring manager's inbox? Most companies use what's called an Applicant Tracking System (ATS). These systems help employers with the recruiting and hiring process. From collecting applications and rating applicants based on predetermined criteria to tracking the communication and interview process, these systems take a lot of the clerical work out of the hiring process.

One of the not-so-secret functions that these systems perform is reviewing the qualifications of an applicant using algorithms. When an employer is receiving hundreds or even thousands of applications, sifting through all of them to find a qualified applicant would be an enormous headache. The algorithms on an ATS are programmed to scan an applicant's resume and cover letter to look for certain keywords, levels of education, and years of experience. Once an application has been vetted, the ATS will rank the applicant and either place their application in the queue to be reviewed by the recruiters or auto-reject the application depending on how the employer has the ATS programmed.

Aside from your application potentially being ranked lower, there's also the chance that your application might get auto-rejected due to a formatting error. If the ATS is unable to read your resume due to a creative font or funky formatting, it may just reject it all together.

So how does having a connection to the company avoid your application being auto-rejected or ranked low on the list? The same way my resume was pulled out of the ATS rejected queue when applying to two of my previous roles. The hiring manager asked the recruiter to keep an eye out for my application after an employee of the company referred me. The recruiter was able to do a search in the ATS and retrieve my application from the rejected queue. Ultimately, I accepted jobs with both of those companies. I imagine it would have gone quite differently had the hiring manager not asked the recruiter to go looking for my application.

Get your resume to the top of the pile

Now that you know an Applicant Tracking System has the ability to rank your application before it is ever viewed by a recruiter or hiring manager, it should come as no surprise that it's possible to have your application ranked incorrectly. Whether it's missing keywords, you don't have the number of years of experience, or whatever the case, your application could be ranked low and be left sitting at the bottom of a pile of hundreds of applications. There are a few ways of improving the chances of having your application ranked higher, but personally I don't recommend relying solely on these as there are many different types of ATSs an employer may use and an endless combination of settings for each of those. Below are a few common recommendations to make your application, resume, and cover letter rank better in an ATS.

Formatting

- Follow formatting and upload instructions on the employer's application portal.
- Use a PDF or docx file format unless otherwise instructed.
- Keep a common and consistent font, such as Arial or Georgia.
- Avoid the use of logos, images, or tables.
- Use a consistent date format when listing your positions and education.

Content

- Update your resume to be specifically tailored to each job you apply for.
- Look for keywords in the job posting and, if appropriate, use them in your resume and cover letter.
- Spell out common abbreviations, such as MBA (Master of Business Administration)

There are also many websites that offer ATS ranking services where you can upload your resume and receive feedback about how to improve its rankings. Personally, I am a big fan of using LinkedIn's ranking features for this. As of the time of this writing, if you sign up for LinkedIn Premium, you gain access to their Competitive Intelligence features that allow you to see your ranking compared to other candidates who applied through LinkedIn. It breaks down your ranking by skills, profile keywords, education, seniority level, and geographic location. These are all statistics employers may use to rank their applicants.

While using these tips and tools to improve your resume, LinkedIn Profile, and application are all well worth your time, ultimately there's no better way to get your resume to the top of the pile than directly connecting with the recruiter or hiring manager. If they're looking for your application, it doesn't matter where it sits in the pile, they'll find it.

Interview as an employee referral

Aside from avoiding having your application rejected or ranked low in the queue, being referred by a current or past employee is one of the best reasons to do whatever you can to find or create a personal connection with the company you are applying to.

There are varying statistics online about the percentage of employee referrals who were offered positions over the past decade compared to unreferred applicants. Almost every statistic shows that for companies that promote employee referrals, these referrals account for around a third of positions filled. Statistics aside, let's look at this from a social perspective.

Have you ever had to hire a caterer, a DJ, or a photographer for a big event like a wedding? Where did you start your search? Of course, you could have just gone online and received endless pages of results. Then you could have called or emailed the companies to ask for quotes. This is your big day though. It's a once-in-a-lifetime event, you're inviting all of your friends and family, and you want to be sure that you are hiring the best.

So, in reality, where do you actually start your search? You likely reach out to friends and family to find out what DJ they hired for their event. You trust the opinion of your friends and family over online search results.

This is exactly the same thing recruiters and hiring managers are thinking when they receive an employee referral for a posted position. Even more than the DJ for your wedding, they have to spend five days a week in the office with this person after they hire them.

Hiring and training also takes time and is very costly. While the cost varies greatly between positions, companies, and industries, I can share an example from a hiring committee I was part of. The interview process alone cost $15,000 per candidate and an additional $25,000 in training on top of the employee's salary to get them through their first three months. The stakes are much higher for the employer than most people realize and having a referral can save them money.

Compound Your Professional Network

I've said it before, and I will say it again: Never stop growing your professional network and never lose touch with the connections you worked so hard to make. *(Sorry for those of you expecting a Ferris Buller quote there.)*

As a college student or young professional, it's easy to be intimidated or discouraged when you lack a well-developed professional network. Unless you were fortunate enough to be born into a family or community well-connected in the industry you're aspiring to, you are likely in the same boat as everyone else your age. Your network is small, you don't have leads to the schools or companies you would like to get connected with, and you don't know where to start. Trust me, you are not alone in that feeling. I have been there multiple times, including just a few years ago during my move to Silicon Valley, and even a few months ago when I decided I wanted to publish this book and didn't know where to start.

The best part about professional networking is watching it compound as you make your way through your career. In high school, you were only connected to your classmates, the people you grew up with, and any organizations you were a part of. In college, your network began to expand rapidly. Depending on the size of the school or university you attended, you joined a community of thousands of current students, alumni, and professors well-established in their fields of study.

However, so did all of your classmates from high school. So, at that point, your network not only grew from the small town you grew up in to the university you attended but expanded all across the country and maybe even the world depending on where all of your high school classmates chose to go to college. This trend only continues to snowball as your career develops and you change jobs and industries.

In high school, I had one connection to an alumnus at Drexel University, a handful of connections to Broadway, and zero connections to the NFL, Disney, Google, or any of their associated industries. By the time I graduated college, I had countless connections at Drexel, many more connections to Broadway, a few dozen connections to the NFL and professional sports industry, two connections to Disney, and maybe one irrelevant connection to Silicon Valley. Fast-forward to six years out of college and my network has grown far beyond the companies and industries I've worked with and now includes professionals on six continents, the International Space Station Communications Team, and a few former classmates working on early developments for the first Mars Mission.

And it's only been one decade since I really started building my professional network. If I can do it, you can too.

 ## SHOW NOTES:

- Take advantage of the countless free resources online for continuing your education. From podcasts and YouTube to free courses offered by the world's most renowned universities, the skills and certifications that will separate you from the rest of the applicants are right at your fingertips.
- Ask yourself: *"What did you do to better yourself while stuck at home in 2020?"* You just may be asked that question in your next job interview.

- Don't focus on what you can't control. Concentrate on what you can control: continuing your education, bettering yourself, and growing your professional network.
- Learn how to *properly* apply for a job. Seek professional help with your resume and cover letter, tailor your resume and cover letter specifically for every job and find or create personal connections with the companies you are applying to.
- Continue growing your professional network even when you are not actively applying for jobs.
- Keep in touch with your university's alumni network. Attend events, share your contact information, and keep your profile up-to-date. Depending on the size of your university, there's a good chance you may find an alumni connection to almost any company or industry you are looking for.

Chapter 16:

Passion is Your Most Powerful Tool

L et's talk about Passion. Passion is something you can't force, learn, or teach. Passion is something that comes naturally, and it's different for everyone. I believe that every person on this planet has the ability to be passionate about something, even if you don't yet know what it is that you are passionate about. Odds are if you are taking the time to read this book, you are passionate about something.

In my opinion, you can be driven to succeed in plenty of areas that you are not genuinely passionate about. Just because you have the drive to do something doesn't mean that it's something you are truly passionate about. Everything has a price, and everything you do in life will take effort. Just getting out of bed in the morning takes effort, but I highly doubt you're passionate about it.

When you like or love to do something and you have a goal in mind, there's likely going to be a mental or physical price you set as your limit—a line you are not willing to cross when chasing those dreams or accomplishing that goal. The mental and physical prices that you have to pay to chase your dreams come in many different forms. For example, if you're an athlete who dreams of going pro, your price is dedicating years of your life—nights, weekends, and holidays—to practicing, conditioning your body, and eating a strict diet. On top of all of that, you're going to undoubtedly experience a ton of rejection. Michael Jordan was famously rejected by his high school's basketball team for not being good enough.

Back in the first decade of the twenty-first century, NASA cut back its programs, halting all human travel to space from US soil. For almost ten years, the United States didn't launch a single manned shuttle into Space. Elon Musk, a Silicon Valley billionaire known for the creation of PayPal and turning Tesla into the car manufacturer with the highest market cap in the world, wanted to take his own bet on space travel. He founded a private space flight company called SpaceX. After 2020, you would have to be living under a rock to not have heard of SpaceX, but it wasn't always that way.

In a famous *60 Minutes* interview back in 2012, Musk was confronted by some of the harshest rejection of his life when his own heroes, including Neil Armstrong and Eugene Cernan, testified in front of the United States congress to speak out against Musk and SpaceX. Armstrong and Cernan, along with other former NASA astronauts, felt that space travel should not be privatized and should be left to NASA and the government. Musk teared up on live TV as he responded to a question about how he felt about his heroes speaking out against the work that he was doing. He responded, "I wish they would come visit ... what I am trying to do is make a significant difference in space flight and make it accessible to almost anyone and I would hope for as much support in that direction as we can receive."

It's not every day that you see a successful billionaire on live TV tear up because his heroes are unsupportive of the work that he is doing. But this rejection did not stop Musk and his team at SpaceX from pursuing their goals. Less than eight years later, on May 30, 2020, Musk and SpaceX in partnership with NASA successfully launched astronauts Robert Benken and Douglas Hurley into orbit, marking the first time in history that a privately developed spacecraft launched astronauts. The launch also marked the first time in nearly a decade that US astronauts launched into space, destined for the International Space Station from US soil.

There is a channel on YouTube I have been following for the past few years. It's a group of guys in their twenties who live in Venice Beach, California and film videos about stepping outside of their comfort zone. Their motto is "seek discomfort," and their channel is called *Yes Theory.* Over the past five years, the Yes Theory team has produced dozens of creative films performing all types of crazy and hilarious stunts and traveling all over the world, usually with less than twenty-four-hour's notice and no plan in mind. Some of their most popular videos have received millions of views, and they have grown an amazing community of fans and followers who frequently will go out of their way to partake in their ongoing effort to say *"yes"* and seek discomfort.

Personally, I've always been a fan of the videos where they match with a girl on Tinder or Bumble and right away ask if she would be willing to go on a first date halfway across the world. Most people, including myself, would never even think about doing something crazy like that, let alone actually pull it off. One of their videos that stuck out to me was one where they heard that their buddy was taking a girl out on a date who he really liked, and they put a call out on social media for all of their California-based fans to caravan down the coast to crash their date. Not only did it make for entertaining content, but it was inspiring how a large group of people with a common goal (even a comedic one) can come together to help each other out, traveling halfway across a state to have a positive impact on two people's lives.

Of all the Yes Theory videos I've watched over the past few years, there's one that stands above them all. In 2019, the Yes Theory crew traveled to Guatemala with a group of other creators to climb a long-lost Mayan pyramid. It was a very well-produced episode, and it was insanely inspiring to see all that they were able to accomplish. This crew of creators traveled to the Guatemalan jungle and proceeded to hike one hundred miles over the span of six days in order to climb this pyramid and help their friend and fellow creator to achieve his dream. It looked absolutely treacherous, but it was definitely a once-in-a-lifetime experience for everyone.

One of the parts I found most inspiring was watching these nerdy creators (who I can associate with) trekking through the jungle completely unprepared (only one of them was a professional hiker). They were battling one-hundred-degree weather, yet they were still retracing their steps, climbing trees, and flying drones in order to get the best shots. On the first day of the hike, they showed the one creator who brought a RED camera with him (Yes, a RED camera in the jungle ... I still have no idea how he carried enough batteries for that thing.) standing on top of another creator's shoulders in the middle of the jungle in order to get the perfect shot.

So why do I bring up Michael Jordan, Elon Musk, and Yes Theory when discussing the need to act on what you are truly passionate about?

As I mentioned before, everything you want to accomplish in life is going to take effort. Everything that takes effort is going to have a price. What separates the goals that you would like to accomplish from the goals that you are driven to accomplish from the goals that you are genuinely passionate about accomplishing is the price you are willing to pay in order to achieve them.

Michael Jordan didn't make into the NBA Hall of Fame after being cut from his high school's basketball team because it was a goal of his. He became the "greatest basketball player ever" because basketball was his true passion, and he was willing to pay any price necessary to get to where he wanted to be.

Elon Musk didn't let the humiliation of his heroes speaking out against him publicly stop him from sending two astronauts into orbit less than eight years later because it was a dream of his. He put his entire heart, soul, and personal bank account into the development and accomplished it because there wasn't a price high enough to stop him from accomplishing what he was passionate about.

The Yes Theory crew and their group of creators didn't risk their lives venturing off-trail, retracing their steps, and consistently going out of their way while hiking one hundred miles through the overgrown Guatemalan jungle in deadly heat to get the perfect shot because they like making videos. They knew no other way of capturing the perfect content to tell the story exactly how they felt they needed to tell it because creating videos that inspire others is their life's passion.

Even if you haven't discovered it yet, once you find out what your passion is, follow it, grab on tight, and get ready for the ride of your life. You'll be amazed at what you can accomplish.

 ## Show Notes:

- Being passionate about something is a gift. Take advantage of it. Your passion will separate you from the rest.
- Don't let what anyone says hold you back from chasing the goals you are passionate about achieving. Your passion is unique to you, and no one else should have a say in how you take advantage of it.

Chapter 17:

Company Meeting

In theatre, we refer to the cast and crew of a show as the "company". At the end of a rehearsal, the director may call for a "company meeting" when they go over all of their notes for the cast and crew. Keeping with the theatrical theme of this book, I only found it appropriate to close out with a *company meeting* to go over all of the director's, blocking, and show notes from the book.

Throughout my education and career, I have had hundreds of moments when I have forced myself to venture outside of my comfort zone in an attempt to make professional connections, whether that meant reaching out to teachers or professors, talking to people at networking events, connecting with professionals on LinkedIn, sending emails, or even walking up to the tech booth at a show. No matter what tactics I've used to meet people, my goal has always been to grow my professional network in hopes that a new connection might pay off one day.

Just like sales, networking is a numbers game. Instead of selling a product, you are marketing yourself to others. In sales, there are always going to be people who are not interested. It could be because the product you are selling is not the right price, is not the right fit, or the customer just may simply not be interested. The same goes for marketing yourself. When you attempt to make new professional connections or apply to a job, you may not have the right skills, the right number of years of experience, or you may not fit the team culture. In sales, every *no* is one step closer to a *yes*. In marketing yourself, every unanswered job application is one step closer to an interview, and every interview is one step closer to a job offer.

You can be the most highly educated and experienced professional in your field, but if you get discouraged and give up after your first rejection, you'll share the same chances of landing that job as the underqualified high school senior filling out the application as part of a school project. The power of persistence plays just as much into professional networking, job applications, and interviews as your education and experience do.

Of the hundreds of conversations, emails, and connection attempts I have made over the last fifteen years, I can narrow the pivotal moments in my entire career down to just two. Think about that. I made hundreds of attempts and only two were required to lead me to companies like Google, Disney, Comcast, and the NFL. Of course, there were plenty of other connections I made during that time, but I can't begin to imagine how different my career journey would be had I not made those two original connections.

The first moment was when I walked up to the producer of the Thanksgiving Day Parade after she spoke to my class during freshman year of college and expressed my interest in volunteering. At that moment, I had absolutely no idea that one sentence was the start of a professional connection that would lead to a series of opportunities toward my career goals.

Had I not volunteered to work that parade, I may have never met the producer from Disney. Had I never met the producer from Disney, I may have not had a connection who was able to refer me when applying. Had I not had a connection when applying, my resume may have never made it through the applicant tracking system, and I may have never been hired. Had I not been hired at Disney, I may not have had the opportunity to grow my broadcast engineering, project management, and customer service skills nor would I have been living in Orlando, and I wouldn't have had the opportunity to meet the people who helped me get hired as the Technical Director at Planet Hollywood. Had I not worked at Planet Hollywood, I may not have made the connections to do freelance work with companies around the country like Microsoft, Tupperware, Coca Cola, and Kohl's. Finally, had I not had four years at Disney on my resume along with an impressive list of freelance work and project management skills, my LinkedIn may not have had the relevant keywords to show up in the search results when the recruiter from Google was looking for candidates.

All of those opportunities started from a single conversation I had my freshman year of college. That's not to say that I wouldn't have come across some of those opportunities had I not had that conversation but connect all the dots and they lead back to that single moment. Around that same time, I was having dozens of conversations and attempting to make new connections, many of which simply didn't pan out. That one conversation with Debbie did though, and there was absolutely no way at that moment that I could have known what it would lead to down the road.

That's just one of my career paths though. Since my freshman year of college, I have been working two parallel career paths that are still moving full speed ahead to this day. The moment that kicked off the other half of my career was the night that my brother and I went to the Phillies game. As we walked around the outfield during the seventh inning stretch, I walked up to that camera operator to find out what it was like working for the team and asked who I could talk to about internship opportunities. Had I not stepped outside of my comfort zone and asked that camera operator for information, I may never have gotten the contact information for the team's producer. Had I not sent multiple unanswered emails to the team's producer, I may not have thought to go on LinkedIn to look for connections to local teams. Had I not found the second-degree connection to the associate producer at the Philadelphia Eagles, I may never have gotten hired with the Eagles. Had I not gotten hired with the Eagles, I may never have discovered my love for the sports broadcast industry. Had I not gotten my foot in the door with the sports broadcast industry in Philadelphia, I may never have made the connections to Comcast Spectator, which led to my time with XFINITY Live, Temple Basketball, Live Nation, Rowan University, Wells Fargo Center, my very successful freelance business fixing AV systems in bars around Philadelphia, and ultimately the connections I needed to land the Audio Visual and Information Technology Manager position on the opening team of the PPL Center.

The avalanche doesn't stop there though. Had I not had the opportunity to grow and prove my skills on the opening of the PPL Center, I would not have been contacted by one of the country's largest NFL Stadiums to interview for the head of broadcasting. Had I not continued to keep my professional network alive in the sports community while I lived in Orlando, I would not have been approached by two MLB stadiums and four NHL arenas with job opportunities. Finally, had I not had that one conversation with the camera operator that night at the Phillies game, I would not have gotten a text message nine years later from the producer who originally hired me at the Philadelphia Eagles, now a Vice President at the San Francisco 49ers, asking if I wanted to freelance for his team when I moved out to California. Had I not accepted the position with my very first boss in sports when he offered to have me join his team in California, I would not have been working down on the field the night that the San Francisco 49ers won the championship game that secured their spot in Super Bowl LIV.

Your entire life is directly impacted by who you know, from the jobs you get offered to how you choose to spend your nights and weekends. The opportunities presented to you and the decisions you make are directly correlated with your personal and professional network.

If you are applying to dozens of jobs and not landing a single interview, it doesn't mean that you're not a qualified candidate. It could be that you simply haven't put in the work necessary to be noticed by those companies. Take a look at who you surround yourself with. Are you surrounded by people you look up to? Do you aspire to be like any of them? Or are you the most successful or driven person you know? You're going to have a hard time growing your professional network and making connections in new industries if you're not surrounding yourself with people who have already made it. This is one of the primary reasons established professionals pay hundreds of thousands of dollars to attend the world's most prestigious MBA programs. Sure, it will look great on their resume to have an MBA from Stanford, but the professional connections they will make during their time in the program can turn out to be even more valuable than anything they actually learn.

One of the recent graduates I mentored was the son of a former coworker of mine. My former coworker reached out to ask me to talk to his son about job application advice. For the story's sake, I'll call him Troy. Troy had applied to dozens of jobs without landing any interviews. After a few months of not hearing back, he started to get discouraged and blame himself. He assumed that he did not have skills or experience necessary and was starting to look into going back to school. This was all I knew about Troy before speaking to him, and I assumed that he was seeking jobs in an overly competitive industry during the 2020 pandemic economy, so his struggle to land an interview made sense to me.

When I called Troy, I asked him what he studied in college and the types of positions he was looking for. I found out that he had a degree in computer science. He had studied and gained experience in JavaScript, Python, Perl, and Shell, along with a slew of additional languages. On top of computer science, Troy's concentration in his undergraduate degree was Artificial Intelligence. This combination of skills was one of the most marketable and highly sought-after skill sets in the job market at the time, especially with big tech companies in Silicon Valley. As if Troy's resume wasn't impressive enough already, he had been partnering with a former professor of his to create a contact tracing application that used artificial intelligence to geographically track users' potential interactions with reported cases of COVID-19.

After just five minutes of chatting with Troy, I was absolutely blown away by his experience and professionalism. He wasn't just brilliant; he was well-spoken, professional, and determined.

You may be wondering at this point what flaws were causing him to not even land interviews. Without asking the question, I already had a pretty good idea of where he was going wrong. I asked Troy what companies he was applying to and how he submitted his applications. He told me that he was using LinkedIn to research and apply for jobs and would occasionally fill out applications on a company website as well.

"Okay, so who have you reached out to at these companies?" I asked.

"Well, I have a buddy who works for a defense contractor, but I don't really have interest in that line of work," he explained.

"Okay, so what about any connections at the companies you are applying to?"

"Well, I don't have any connections to those companies."

Bingo, he provided the exact excuse I expected.

I explained that he should use LinkedIn to search for second-degree connections with the companies he is applying to. We drafted a few template messages he could send to recruiters, and we discussed methods to establish connections with companies he was aiming to land interviews with. Each idea I floated by him he admitted he had never thought of doing. None of these were groundbreaking ideas:

- Reaching out to recruiters on LinkedIn
- Looking for second-degree connections
- Connecting with the alumni organization at his alma mater
- Reaching out to his former professors
- Searching for contact information on company websites

Aside from trying to make the connections with the companies and grow his network, we spoke about how he could make his application stand out. I shared the story about what my high school principal told me to do when applying to colleges I didn't meet the minimum requirements for and told Troy to create a portfolio of his work. Having strong technical and programming skills, he was able to create a stunning website that featured the projects he worked on in college along with the contact tracing application he and his former professor were developing. Once the website was built, he added a link to the site on his cover letter, resume, and job applications.

After meeting with Troy a few times, I felt that I knew him well enough to offer to be a reference for him as well. I told him if he ever came across a position at one of the companies I was connected with, I would be happy to submit his name. In the end, Troy went from being a top applicant who was simply unable to get his application to the top of the pile to being a highly sought-after applicant with competing job offers because he was able to effectively market himself and his skills.

Troy is a brilliant young professional who will be a prime candidate for dozens of the most well-known companies across the world. I guarantee he's going to be making six figures in his first job, and he won't make it two years with his first company before he starts to get competing bids.

Troy did everything right. He got a solid education, he worked to grow his skills outside of school, and he sought help when he was unable to get the attention of the employers. The one area that Troy failed to plan for—at no fault of his own—was marketing himself. Troy is a classic example of a young professional who was taught book smarts in school while his education completely left out the functional street skills necessary to put his book smarts to work.

You can be the best applicant for a job, check every box on the description requirements, and have the best-looking cover letter and resume in the stack, but if you can't get your resume to the top of the pile, you've got as much of a chance of landing the position as everyone else who's less qualified.

Throughout this book, I talk a lot about the key jobs I held with some of the bigger-name companies. I mention a few of the lesser-known places as well, but I don't go deep into detail about the sheer number of jobs I have applied for and interviewed with over the years. I don't want this book to glorify my career and sound like I simply had a few lucky breaks. I will absolutely admit that being in the right place at the right time played a large role in a few of the opportunities presented to me over the years, but had I not acted on any of those opportunities, being in the right place at the right time wouldn't have done me any good. For every opportunity that I had throughout my career, there were at least a dozen opportunities that didn't pan out.

I can go back and recall how I landed every single interview and offer over the years. This includes full-time and part-time jobs, short term contracts, and freelance work. Here are a few examples:

- Six Flags Great Adventure: Didn't apply, had a connection through my high school
- Ritz Theatre Company: Didn't apply, called technical directors all around town and was offered the job over the phone
- CBS Radio Internship: Applied, called the news desk to follow up, interviewed, and was offered the position

- Fringe Arts Philadelphia: Didn't apply, had a connection through college and they created a position for me
- Philadelphia Eagles: Didn't apply, connected with the associate producer through a connection on LinkedIn, offered an internship followed by a contract
- XFINITY Live! Philadelphia: Didn't apply, walked up to the DJ booth on my twenty-first birthday to strike up a conversation with the tech guy, hired a week later
- PPL Center Arena: Applied, made over four dozen phone calls to connections in three states, followed up for almost two months, interviewed, followed up for another month while I waited for an answer, got offered the job
- Walt Disney World: Reached out to a professional connection at the company first, was told to share my resume with him, he shared my resume with the department that was hiring, was emailed by said department and told to apply to get my name in the system, interviewed with a three-question interview two weeks later, then offered the job
- Planet Hollywood: Didn't apply, was introduced to the general manager, had an informal meeting, then was offered the job
- Dozens of corporate keynotes across the United States: Didn't apply, was called by producers who had received my name as a referral, offered the contract jobs
- Google: Didn't apply, was contacted by a recruiter, went through an intense interview process, then was offered the job
- San Francisco 49ers: Didn't apply, received a text from my former boss when he heard I was moving into the area, offered the contract job

Of all of the positions I have listed above, I *applied* to one of them: the CBS Radio internship my senior year of high school. For every single one of the other positions I have held in my career to this day, including the many not listed above, I got my foot in the door through professional connections. Even in situations where I didn't have any direct connections to the company I was applying for, I was persistent in my search to establish connections to get my foot in the door.

Now, as I mentioned above, for every opportunity that I did get, there were dozens that I didn't. Here are a few notable mentions: *Please note, these are all wonderful companies and I am only mentioning them for the sake of the lesson. I have absolutely no hard feelings about not being hired by any of them.*

- The Philadelphia Phillies: Applied four times, sent dozens of emails, had more than fifteen professional connections who worked for the organization, never got an interview
- The Philadelphia Flyers and 76ers: Applied a total of eight times, exchanged more than thirty emails, got invited to one interview, never offered a job
- NBC Universal: Applied twelve times to positions in New York and Orlando, interviewed twice, offered a position for less than $11.00 per hour, turned it down
- Walt Disney Imagineering: Applied a total of twenty-one times, exchanged more than 150 emails over five years, had thirteen interviews, two follow-up interviews, and zero offers

As of 2020, I can look back in my inbox and see that I have applied to more than 250 jobs since I opened my first email account in 2005. With 250 applications, I've had about seventy-five interviews, a few dozen follow-ups, and about fifteen that panned out to offers, of which I've accepted less than five. That's a 2 percent rate of return.

As of the time of this writing, I am still under the age of twenty-nine with a long career ahead of me. While these days I tend to be contacted by recruiters about half a dozen times each month thanks to the size of my professional network and notable companies on my resume, just like the top actors on Broadway, I am still guaranteed to have plenty of years of unanswered applications, emails, and rejections ahead of me. Rejection is part of life, and there is absolutely nothing that you can do to avoid it other than not taking any risks. I don't know about you, but that sounds like a pretty boring way to live your life. You can be scared of rejections, try to avoid them, and let the fear of them play into every decision you make each day—or you can learn and grow from them.

To my readers, if there is one key lesson I hope that you take away from this book, it's this: ***Don't let the fear of rejection or the feeling of discouragement hold you back from chasing your dreams.*** No matter what anybody tells you, you are absolutely capable of achieving your craziest goals and aspirations. It will probably take years of hard work and dedication, overcoming roadblocks, blood, sweat, tears, and rejection, but if you have that burning passion within you and don't allow anyone or anything to diminish it, you absolutely can succeed.

- Never stop learning
- Never stop growing
- Never stop meeting new people
- Never lose touch with who you truly are
- Never stop giving back
- Never apply to a job without reaching out
- Don't forget those who helped you along the way

Now, get up and go!

Curtain Call:

It Takes a Community

I wouldn't have a chance of being where I am today without the love, leadership, and guidance of all the family, friends, and mentors who have had such a strong impact on my life. Thank you all. I am forever indebted to your love, lessons, and kindness.

Mom, Dad, and Michael

Uncle Rich, Adrienne, Matt & Ryan

My whole family

Dan S.

Don G.

Gary M.

Joe D.

Dr. Robert K.

Paul T.

Mikey L.

Deb V.

Kristine M.

Bill B.

Dr. Michael M.

Dr. Ron M.

Nick R.

Brian M.

Larry E.

Dr. David R.

Dr. John C.

Jimmy H.

Emmy L.

Aron K.

David S.

Fran R.

Denise F.

Brian K.

Dan B.

Mark W.

Gene H.

Frank M.

Mark E.

Bob T.

Nick M.

Jason S.

Derek H.

Debbie L.

Todd M.

Eric L.

Chuck T.

Erica M.

Steve G.

Rick A.

Paul C.

Aubrey K.

Morgan James Publishing

About the Author

From performing on stage to directing and designing set and technical elements for musicals, **Brett Axler** knew he had marketable skills that could take him further than eight shows a week on Broadway. After discovering his passion for nighttime spectaculars at Disney, Brett pursued his dreams of working for Disney before finding out that his skills were far more lucrative in industries outside of entertainment. During his freshman year of college, by total accident, he landed his first big gig with the NFL as a broadcast engineer for the Philadelphia Eagles before being hired on to half a dozen other sports teams and media networks by his senior year of college. Brett's whirlwind career continued as he was hired to lead the opening of a

280-million-dollar professional sports arena, produce more than two dozen shows throughout Philadelphia and New York, and was eventually pursued by his original dream employer, Disney. He spent four years working for Disney Parks Live Entertainment in Orlando, Florida while freelancing as a technical director for corporate events around the country which led to his most recent endeavor as a Project Manager for Google in Silicon Valley. Brett currently resides in Mountain View, CA.

What's Next?

For press inquiries, coaching calls, mentorships, and speaking engagements, please visit: www.BrettAxler.com or email Brett at brett@brettaxler.com

A free ebook edition is available with the purchase of this book.

To claim your free ebook edition:

1. Visit MorganJamesBOGO.com
2. Sign your name CLEARLY in the space
3. Complete the form and submit a photo of the entire copyright page
4. You or your friend can download the ebook to your preferred device

A **FREE** ebook edition is available for you or a friend with the purchase of this print book.

CLEARLY SIGN YOUR NAME ABOVE

Instructions to claim your free ebook edition:
1. Visit MorganJamesBOGO.com
2. Sign your name CLEARLY in the space above
3. Complete the form and submit a photo of this entire page
4. You or your friend can download the ebook to your preferred device

Print & Digital Together Forever.

Snap a photo   Free ebook   Read anywhere